# African Youth
# on the Information Highway

## Participation and Leadership
## in Community Development

*edited by Osita Ogbu and Paschal Mihyo*

INTERNATIONAL DEVELOPMENT RESEARCH CENTRE
Ottawa • Cairo • Dakar • Johannesburg • Montevideo • Nairobi • New Delhi • Singapore

Published by the International Development Research Centre
PO Box 8500, Ottawa, ON, Canada K1G 3H9

Legal deposit: 2nd quarter 2000
National Library of Canada
ISBN 0-88936-914-3

The catalogue of IDRC Books and this publication may be consulted online
at http://www.idrc.ca/booktique.

# CONTENTS

**Foreword** — *Eva M. Rathgeber* . . . . . . . . . . . . . . . . . . . . . . . . . . . . . v

**Acknowledgments** . . . . . . . . . . . . . . . . . . . . . . . . . . . . . . . . . . . . . ix

**Executive Summary** . . . . . . . . . . . . . . . . . . . . . . . . . . . . . . . . . . . xi

**Chapter 1**
A Youth Leadership Program for Africa
— *Paschal B. Mihyo and Osita Ogbu* . . . . . . . . . . . . . . . . . . . . . . 1

**Chapter 2**
Technical Feasibility of Implementing ALPID
— *Muriuki Mureithi* . . . . . . . . . . . . . . . . . . . . . . . . . . . . . . . . . . 23

**Chapter 3**
Implementing ALPID in Kenya: Stakeholders and Coordination
— *Kadzo Kogo* . . . . . . . . . . . . . . . . . . . . . . . . . . . . . . . . . . . . . . 55

**Chapter 4**
Implementing ALPID in Uganda: Challenges and Possibilities
— *Agnes Katama* . . . . . . . . . . . . . . . . . . . . . . . . . . . . . . . . . . . . 75

**Chapter 5**
Electronic Networking in Uganda: Building Local Support Capacity Through
Youth Volunteers
— *Charles Musisi* . . . . . . . . . . . . . . . . . . . . . . . . . . . . . . . . . . . . 89

**Chapter 6**
Implementing ALPID in Africa: Conclusions and Recommendations
— *Muriuki Mureithi* . . . . . . . . . . . . . . . . . . . . . . . . . . . . . . . . . . 95

# CONTENTS

**Appendix 1**

Acronyms and Abbreviations . . . . . . . . . . . . . . . . . . . . . . . . . . . . . 105

**Appendix 2**

List of Workshop Participants . . . . . . . . . . . . . . . . . . . . . . . . . . . 107

# FOREWORD

In sub-Saharan Africa (SSA) today, about 80% of the population is under 30 years old. This percentage continues to rise, but employment opportunities for young people are severely limited. The structural-adjustment policies of the 1980s and 1990s have led to reductions in the absolute number of jobs available in the public sector. The private sector in most African countries has grown slowly and has been unable to absorb the large numbers of school leavers and graduates who annually flood the market. In fact, the informal sector accounts for up to 80% of gross domestic product in some African countries.

However, the bright side of economic restructuring and accelerated change is that it also presents youth with new opportunities. Among these is the emergence of informal sectors and small and medium-sized enterprises (SMEs), both of which demand new types of skills. Enterprise and entrepreneurship education and learning, a fairly new field, is responding to a call for new attitudes, knowledge, and skills, preparing young people to meet the emerging demands of labour markets and livelihood opportunities.

One of the most promising areas for youth is information and communications technologies (ICTs). ICTs are for everyone, young and old, but perhaps it is the young who must lead the way. The International Development Research Centre (IDRC) has been working on ICT issues since the 1970s and has helped many African institutions establish bibliographic centres and information retrieval systems. IDRC was an early supporter of PADIS (Pan African Documentation and Information System) at the Economic Commission for Africa, based in Addis Ababa, Ethiopia, and currently supports the Publication and Information Centre, HealthNet, and an electronic network, all based at Makerere University, Kampala, Uganda.

In 1996, IDRC made a decision to use ICTs more effectively to accelerate development in SSA. Instead of focusing on our traditional partners — universities, government ministries, and research institutions — we decided to work directly with target communities to ensure that they would be more immediately brought into the development process. In this context, we launched the Acacia Initiative as an international effort to empower SSA communities to apply ICTs in their own social and economic development.

In all probability, ICTs are here to stay, and they will increasingly become a part of everyday life in Africa, as has happened in other parts of the world. The youth of Africa will be prime players in linking the continent to the information highway. One of the objectives of this workshop[1] was to explore ways to make this happen.

The three main objectives of Acacia are as follows:

- To examine how SSA communities can use information and communication to solve local social and economic development problems;

- To learn from and record this knowledge and disseminate it widely; and

- To involve others (international organizations, donors, the private sector, national governments, and nongovernmental organizations) in using ICTs to increase community access to information and communication.

In all this, IDRC wants to ensure that youth have a prominent role, not only as users of information (or as people being acted on), but also as decision-makers in the processes of development in their own communities. Our focus in this initiative is on assisting rural communities to become a part of national development processes by facilitating their access to information and knowledge and by providing them with opportunities to share their own insights, knowledge, and experience with their urban compatriots. IDRC also puts special emphasis on the involvement of women and girls.

The whole world is on the brink of a major reconceptualization of how we live and work together. Countries that only a decade or two ago seemed remote now have the potential to be active partners in global development. ICTs offer African youth the opportunity to bring their views and perspectives to a wider

---

[1] Youth Leadership Programme for Information and Communication Technologies for Community Development in Africa (ALPID) Workshop, 2–3 March 1998, Safari Park Hotel, Nairobi, Kenya.

audience. The three areas of focus endorsed at this workshop — SMEs, health, and land use and environmental management — seem to me to offer particularly good potential for youth input. But more important, ICTs offer African youth the opportunity to actively participate in the development of their communities and countries by sharing their knowledge, enthusiasm, and creativity with their fellow countrymen and countrywomen.

**Eva M. Rathgeber**
*Regional Director, Eastern and Southern Africa*
*International Development Research Centre*

# ACKNOWLEDGMENTS

We wish to acknowledge the generous financial support for this workshop from the management group of the International Development Research Centre (IDRC). In particular, we wish to register our appreciation for the encouragement we received from Eva Rathgeber and Rob Valantin, who supported this idea from the very beginning.

Within IDRC Nairobi, George Githembe, Joy Mita, Joanne Mwenda, and Edith Ofwona worked tirelessly to ensure the success of the workshop. George, Edith, and Mwihaki Kimura (also of IDRC) took responsibility for following up with the workshop proceedings. Their efforts helped shape the outcome. We also thank Aminah Kasinga for excellent facilitation during the workshop. She kept us focused on its objectives and helped us flush out the most important aspects of the youth program.

We are grateful to all the workshop participants, whose enthusiasm for the program enriched the discussions and debates. The participants worked long into the night during the working-group sessions, and we acknowledge their dedication.

# EXECUTIVE SUMMARY

## Introduction to ALPID

The principal objectives of a proposed Youth Leadership Program for Information and Communication Technologies and Community Development in Africa (ALPID) are the following:

- To use skilled youth volunteers to train and popularize the use and absorption of information and communication technologies (ICTs) in various producer, service, and administrative communities in Africa; and

- To collect, store, and disseminate information on development needs and achievements, from these communities.

Through these processes, communities will learn to use ICTs to improve their capacity for decision-making on development issues. Through ICTs, they will have opportunities to upgrade their indigenous systems and knowledge in the areas of health, small and medium-sized enterprises (SMEs), and land use and environmental management.

ALPID is based on the principle that youth can be employed as vehicles of change for existing and emerging technologies in communities where lack of access to information constitutes a binding constraint on development potential. Established youth-to-community education programs have had successful impacts and have contributed to the quality of life in Africa, indicating that youth can be useful agents of change. Youth have quickly adapted to using information technology (IT), and many adults are already learning IT skills from younger members of their societies.

ALPID is to be implemented as a subtheme within the Acacia Initiative. Under Acacia, ALPID is designed to contribute to the development of sub-Saharan Africa (SSA) by facilitating the timely flow of information for decision-making in rural communities. ALPID will test the proposition that ICTs can have as significant a transformational effect in the developing world as they have had in developed economies. If rural communities in Africa use ICTs to their own ends, they may be able to shift some decision-making away from metropolitan centres and international development organizations and back to their own communities, where the development challenges are most acutely felt. The initial target countries will be Kenya, Nigeria, Tanzania, and Uganda; however, the workshop discussions focused on the three East African countries: Kenya, Tanzania, and Uganda.

Acacia aims to achieve three mutually reinforcing goals that combine to promote equitable, sustainable, and self-directed development in disadvantaged and rural communities in SSA:

- To discover and demonstrate the ability of disadvantaged SSA communities, especially women and youth, to use information and communication to solve local development problems;

- To learn from Acacia's research and experience and disseminate this knowledge widely; and

- To foster international interest and involvement in using ICTs to support rural community development, thereby increasing community access to information and communication.

Critical issues for the program include ensuring project sustainability after donor resources are exhausted, focusing on rural communities, using appropriate technology, and incorporating youth into the program. Workshop participants critically analyzed these issues during the presentations and working-group discussions.

## The East African context

Four papers at the workshop were on ICT development in East Africa. They gave an overview of the existing ICT infrastructure and its national distribution in ALPID's target countries, as well as discussing the policy environment in these countries and the impacts of these policies on ICT development. Finally, they considered the feasibility of increasing ICT applications in rural communities.

The presentations indicated that these countries have some aspects of ICT development and evolution in common. For instance, although all these countries have ICT infrastructure, this is of far lower quality and quantity than the world average. Teledensity ranges from a low of 0.23 per 100 people to a high of 0.98, in Uganda and Kenya, respectively. Personal-computer (PC) density is closer to 0 per 100 people than 1 per 100 people, and the annual rate of telephone failures is as high as 191 faults per 100 lines in certain areas. In 1995, the comparable world average teledensity was 12.14 per 100 people; PC density, 4.23 per 100 people; and telephone failure rate, 28.8 faults per 100 lines. The ALPID target countries also show a wide disparity in national ICT-infrastructure distribution, largely to the disadvantage of the rural populations. In each target country, the rural population constitutes on average 80% of the national population but shares fewer than 20% of all telephones. In many areas, these countries have no telephone systems at all. Lack of other supporting infrastructure in the rural areas (such as commercial power, support and maintenance facilities for ICTs, and training) exacerbates the already poor availability of ICT infrastructure and its use. Low income levels in rural areas, coupled with higher operating costs, further disadvantage the rural populations.

Yet, it is now accepted that the use of ICTs would have a profound impact on rural communities by enabling them to make better informed decisions. It is therefore imperative that ICTs be extended to these areas. New technologies are available to extend ICTs, particularly telecommunications, to rural areas. These include radio-based technologies for datacasting, data over high-frequency radio, and stationary and mobile satellite communications. Technology is not the problem. The problem is government policies inhospitable to ICT development, combined with the economics of extending ICTs to rural areas vis-à-vis the ability to pay for services. Another major challenge is illiteracy, which affects the ability of rural communities to effectively harness ICT facilities. For ALPID to succeed, it has to be anchored in a sociopolitical environment that fosters the development of ICTs, with emphasis on the development of rural areas. At the time of the workshop, all the ALPID target countries were reforming their ICT sectors and creating structures to support rural access to ICTs. Uganda and Tanzania, especially, have made advances in this regard.

ALPID will apply ICTs in its thematic areas through information bureaus (telecentres), which should be anchored in national programs to ensure synergy and sustainability. For example, in Kenya, land use should be linked to the Agricultural Sector Improvement Programme; health for rural communities should be related to the Community Based Health Information Service, which is promoted by the African Medical and Research Foundation and IDRC; and SMEs should be linked to trade-information dissemination mechanisms being established by the

Kenya National Chamber of Commerce and Industry and the Export Promotion Council.

From 1991 to 1995, Makerere University, Kampala (MUKLA), Uganda, alone provided e-mail services within Uganda and East Africa. In 1995, Uganda pioneered the full use of Internet services in the region. Today, MUKLA continues to deliver reliable links with a global reach to government, business, international agencies, community groups, and nongovernmental organizations. It was a founding member of the East African Internet Association and the Internet Society of Uganda.

Private-sector companies in Kenya are now exploiting ICTs in commercial activities. A presentation from Media Street (a private firm), including a practical demonstration on the use of the Internet in commercial applications, was very helpful. The workshop was informed that a group of Kenyan companies (Shell BP, Document Handling Limited [DHL], Securicor, and Media Street) had formed a consortium to pioneer e-commerce in Kenya. Media Street is maintaining a website (www.eastafrica.com), and the other companies are responsible for distributing purchased goods, internationally (DHL) and locally (Securicor). The goods are distributed through petrol stations across the country (Shell and BP). One advantage of e-commerce is the direct contact it affords between traders and consumers, which eliminates intermediaries who do not add value to the final product. The consortium is considering setting up communication centres in petrol stations to facilitate public access to the Internet.

A presentation by Mr Ali Mfuruki, from Infotech Tanzania, offered insight into the status of ICT development in Tanzania. The Tanzanian telecommunication network is poor, with a teledensity of 0.3, and unevenly distributed. The policy and regulatory framework had changed in the four years since sector reform began. Customers now have a choice of services from a competitive market, largely dictated by market forces. Consequently, Tanzania has three Internet access providers (IAPs) (Datel, WilKen, and Sita), serving 13 Internet service providers, who in turn serve 2000 dial-up clients. Licencing of IAPs in Tanzania is restrictive, which affects the pricing of Internet services. The Tanzania Communication Commission restricts the number of licences to three and requires a fee of 100 000 United States dollars (USD) for each licence. This is a barrier to competitive Internet services, as it transfers the financial burden to the customer.

Other services in Tanzania (such as cellular telephony, datacasting, paging, and broadcasting) are now provided competitively, with prices much lower than in other ALPID countries. Computer density is even lower, at 0.3%. High taxation on hardware, at 32%, is cited as a major obstacle. The greatest problem is not the structural weakness of the sector but a low-performing economy and therefore affordability to citizens. Per capita income is 200 USD, so basic ICT facilities are way beyond the reach of the majority.

Based on the presentations and the discussions on the floor, it was agreed that ALPID will focus on disadvantaged communities, where ICTs are not often available. For making progress on extending the infrastructure, an ICT-friendly environment is critical. An enabling environment for fast development of the telecommunication sector was already in place in both Tanzania and Uganda because of government-implemented sector-reform programs. Kenya, in contrast, had yet to undertake sector reform. It was noted, however, that the Kenyan government had published documentation on policy reform in the telecommunication sector and was expected to establish a new regulatory framework by 1998. In the meantime, satellite technology, such as Very Small Aperture Terminals (VSATs), could not be used in Kenya to serve the rural areas, as the government had policy restrictions on such technologies.

In none of these three countries did the workshop participants report barriers on the importation or use of IT. Taxation was high in Tanzania (32%), which affected affordability, but Kenya had lowered the import duty on computers to only 5%. In addition, the introduction of computer education in Kenyan secondary schools was giving IT development a big boost. However, commercial power was unavailable in most rural areas, and even where it was available outages and voltage fluctuations occurred frequently. Solar power was becoming a feasible alternative, and the Kenya Posts and Telecommunications Corporation was using it extensively to power small rural exchanges.

Workshop participants recommended that in places where telephone land lines are unavailable, other technologies should be evaluated on a case-by-case basis. These would include high-frequency radio, extensively used by relief agencies in relief operations; datacasting over radio or television broadcast signals or via satellite; mobile communications, including cellular radio, in areas with coverage; mobile trunk radio; global mobile personal communication systems; satellite VSATs, where allowed by the regulatory authorities; and offline technologies, such as audiovisual and audio tapes, floppy diskettes, and CD-ROMs.

A number of constraints still inhibit the use of ICTs, the most marked being that target countries have low per capita incomes. A modem costs as much as the average annual income of a citizen of the region. At the end of 1995, per capita incomes in Kenya, Tanzania, and Uganda were 267, 124, and 244 USD, respectively, whereas the price of a modem ranged from 200 to 280 USD. Other constraints include high illiteracy levels. The human–technology interface also needs to be addressed, because many people do not know how to operate the ICTs and find the technology intimidating. Workshop participants emphasized the need for training, specifically to teach technical and communication skills in the target communities.

Youth volunteers will need to have good research, communication, and social skills to effectively carry out their responsibilities. By applying these skills, in combination with their knowledge of their particular sectors, the volunteers will be able to design and package community-based information systems to help the communities identify resources within their environments and use them for self-advancement. To effectively transfer knowledge to adults, the youth volunteers will have to be familiar with methods of adult learning.

Graduates of the ALPID program will become new role models in the communities through their work in transferring knowledge to the adults. The youth will become involved in various management roles in the program, from the initial needs assessment, to information dissemination, to management of the information bureaus (Box 1). It will be important to combat high turnover rates. As graduates, the volunteers will be looking for permanent jobs, and if good opportunities come up they might leave the program midstream. A competitive package must be included as an incentive to stay. The package could include training opportunities or perhaps some remuneration that is within the salary structure of the implementing partners.

Graduates leave public universities in Kenya at around 25 years of age, which is outside the range initially proposed for ALPID. The age bracket therefore needs to be reconsidered. It was noted that the lower age limit would bring in youth not who do not yet have the necessary skills, but the upper limit would have to include people looking for future job opportunities and beginning to look for professional stability.

Youth representatives at the workshop expressed support for the program and saw ALPID as an opportunity to repay the community. An example of a youth contribution to society and self-development cited at the workshop is Mesh Mentors, a group in Uganda that champions the role of the graduate youth volunteer in community development, focusing primarily on women.

All three countries have problems that ALPID could address, and they each have basic ICT infrastructure and a large pool of youth. Kenya, for example, is

Box 1

**A personal experience**

One of the participants representing the youth (Virginia Ruguru) gave a personal account of her experience in a youth volunteer program in 1997:

- Training, 1 month;
- Adaptation to the community, 4 months;
- Full deployment in the community, 6 months; and
- Transition back to parent or implementing institution, 2 months.

The remuneration was 6 000 KES per month, together with housing and medical coverage (in 2000, 74.35 Kenyan shillings [KES] = 1 United States dollar [USD]).

---

already implementing complementary programs that could help anchor ALPID. Tanzania and Uganda are creating ICT-friendly policy environments, and both countries have very specific programs to develop telecommunications in the rural areas and have set up funds to support ICT development in such areas, indicating a readiness to engage in the ALPID program.

Certain crosscutting issues for the program were identified. The youth in Africa do not constitute a homogeneous group, and one will need to observe a gender balance when selecting youth to run the program. In selecting the core focus of ALPID activities, one will need to ensure that the operational area is chosen to promote gender equity. In farming, for example, women would be disadvantaged by programs focusing on cash crops, as this is an area in which men have more interest and control. The workshop noted that in practice women are under societal pressures arising from pregnancy, marriage, etc., that negatively affect gender equity in volunteer programs in the long run. The method of information delivery should be carefully selected. It was noted that in the rural areas the radio is man's domain, and women have limited access to radio as a source of information. The introduction of new technology should be implemented equitably. Workshop participants also stressed the need to include measures to assure sustainability. Cost-based services should be encouraged. The returns to the user community should rise progressively, in line with increasing awareness and use. Where possible, cheaper technology, which is easier to maintain locally, should be used. In all cases, ALPID should use existing infrastructure to reduce costs, and it should work in partnership with active government programs.

If the program is to be successful, it must fully address the needs of the community. A complete needs assessment must be carried out to ascertain community priorities. Where the community is fully sensitized, it should be prepared to provide counterpart resources (for example, physical infrastructure or even volunteer services). Community support is necessary to sustain the program and is a direct indication of the program's usefulness to the community. Workshop participants stressed the need for continuous monitoring and evaluation and the use of outcomes to continuously improve and adjust the program.

## Thematic areas and recommendations

ALPID will target support to firms in the SME category that have 3–50 employees. Such firms exhibit high growth rates, have a high level of employment generation, constitute about 70% of regional local enterprises, and have extensive presence in rural Africa. Support will be extended through telecentres in major towns and in areas close to, or linked to, technology nodes. ALPID should take into account the high mobility of the enterprises.

The fields targeted in the health sector are adolescent health and sexuality; and preventive and curative health care. The main sites for implementation will be underserved areas with highly transient communities, such as border and fishing communities. The working-group reports highlighted these in more detail.

Considering the region's high dependence on agriculture, workshop participants emphasized a focus on the land-use sector as a way to increase agricultural productivity and farm incomes and protect the environment through sound ecological management. The participants highlighted the importance of using indigenous knowledge, as well as the need for information on weather and climate patterns, farming techniques, farm production, storage methods for farm produce, and market information.

The initial steps for successful implementation will be to prepare a comprehensive project document for ALPID, taking into account the workshop proceedings; secure funding for the project; and identify project partners. Being a regional project, ALPID should find partners with regional reach or, where this is impossible, partners with extensive national activity. Soliciting ideas for a needs assessment from professionals within the thematic areas is essential. Finally, establishing an operational framework for community sensitization will ensure good takeoff for the project.

CHAPTER 1

# A YOUTH LEADERSHIP PROGRAM FOR AFRICA

*Paschal B. Mihyo and Osita Ogbu*

## Introduction

This chapter introduces a youth volunteer program for information and communication technologies (ICTs) for communities in Africa. The program, known as the Youth Leadership Program for Information and Communication Technologies and Community Development in Africa (ALPID), derives its impetus from the realization that information gaps and lack of access to existing informatics will further marginalize Africa as we enter the 21st century. The serious dichotomies between urban and rural areas and between formal and informal sectors delineate where the needs are greatest and the likely constituency for this program.

This program will bring together youth from participating countries of Africa, Europe, and North America. We can rely on youth, who are usually agents of change, to act as harbingers of the Information Age, bringing existing and emerging technologies into communities, activities, or sectors where lack of access to information has undermined and constrained development efforts. In connection with this program, the term *community* refers to a group of people residing, working, or associating together in a given location and linked functionally or residentially. Such communities could be residential, occupational, educational, or health-, production-, or service-oriented. In sectors such as health, microenterprises, and environmental management, information can contribute to optimal outcomes, and the program we articulate below pays special attention to these areas of great importance to Africa.

## Underlying principles

Our proposal is based on the following fundamental principles:

- That youth have been critical to the propagation of community knowledge and have a big influence on their parents and other adults in their communities;

- That through youth-to-youth and youth-to-community education programs, the youth have (even at a tender age) succeeded in helping to improve the quality of life in Africa where others have failed;

- That status and other problems tend to constrain adult-to-adult education programs, whereas youth-to-adult education programs do not have such problems;

- That the youth have shown leadership in acquiring the skills needed to use ICTs and that most adults are already learning these skills from young members of the community (we need to structure and organize this transfer of skills at the community level);

- That the youth, as agents of ICTs, would have a unique opportunity to give back to society a bit of what society has given them in terms of their care and education;

- That most youth in Africa have been systematically alienated from their communities through education and that through such community-based programs they can be reintegrated into their communities and be given an opportunity to engage in community development;

- That for community-based programs to succeed, they must recognize, respect, and reciprocate with community systems of knowledge, power, and production;

- That the national youth service programs of various governments have laid the foundations for the integration of the youth into their communities and that a youth-to-community education program for information-technology (IT) literacy would add a greater value to the role of youth in community development; and

- That "information poverty" is at the core of Africa's slow recovery and stagnation and that equipping youth with IT skills and proper methodologies to transfer such skills to adults involved in production and services can go a long way toward spearheading Africa's entry into the global information society.

# Objectives of the program

The main objective of the program is to use skilled youth volunteers to train and popularize the use and absorption of ICTs in various producer, service, and administrative communities in Africa. We will attain this objective by placing the youth at the centre of this development process.

## Specific objectives

The project seeks to achieve the following:

- To enable communities to improve their capacity for decision-making on development issues by increasing their capacity to use the new ICTs;

- To enable the youth to participate in community development;

- To provide an opportunity for communities to use the new ICTs to upgrade their indigenous systems and knowledge in the areas of health and production;

- To provide an opportunity for communities to use the new ICTs to upgrade their traditional information systems and networks; and

- To create information packages and databases of indigenous knowledge and systems of production, environmental management, and indigenous technologies.

# The problematique and its justification

The conventional view of knowledge transfer is that knowledge is best transferred from adults to youth or from adults to adults. Even liberal educators who attempt to use participatory, or Socratic, methods of learning have jealously guarded the elderly image of the teacher. Even in peer tutoring, older or smarter youths have been used as substitutes for teachers. Only in evangelical preaching have youth been easily accepted as capable of transferring their knowledge without impersonating their elders. But even here, youth who preach are assumed to be gifted.

Societal prejudices have sustained these conservative views on the capabilities of youth. In most communities, young people are assumed to be unsure of what they want, short-tempered, lacking in coping skills, immature, restless, unsettled, and unable to handle stress. Because of these prejudices, youth have not been given more responsibility or a chance to use their potential to the maximum.

These prejudices have had dire consequences for development processes in Africa. Elders who have maintained their right to be educators have been unable to update themselves in various areas. Most of their views and skills have remained static. The youth, on the contrary, have been acquiring knowledge and skills that they have had difficulty transferring to their elders and their communities. As a result, communities have failed to be transformed by the educational systems and institutions around them. The youth have been relevant to all other institutions except their communities.

A related problem is that of mutual irrelevance. Because adult skills have remained static, they have become irrelevant to the youth, and the youth have acquired some new and dynamic skills that their communities have not completely internalized, because these skills have remained in the youth sectors of society. This mutual irrelevance has widened the divide between the modern sectors and the indigenous sectors and slowed the processes of mutual enrichment. For this reason, education has continued to benefit more and more people in the modern sectors while the so-called traditional sectors have fallen further and further behind. In the past two decades, however, the myth of adult monopoly over knowledge and the mechanisms of its transfer has been shattered. Youth-to-youth schools have sprung up in Angola, Benin, Botswana, Burkina Faso, Cameroon, the Congo (Kinshasa), Ghana, Kenya, Lesotho, Liberia, Malawi, Niger, Nigeria, Rwanda, Senegal, Sierra Leone, South Africa, Tanzania, Togo, Zambia, and Zimbabwe.

Youth volunteers, working with the help of teachers and other specialists, have become very effective in the areas of health, nutrition, safety, sanitation, and environmental management. In Zambia, for example, the youth have helped to popularize immunization for polio, measles, diphtheria, TB, etc. Using songs and poems composed by young people, the youth have easily changed other youths' and the community's attitudes toward immunization (Otaala 1986[1]). In Botswana, Zambia, and Zimbabwe, youth have spearheaded community programs on clean water and sanitation, good diets and nutrition, and the prevention of diarrhea. They use songs and demonstrations, plays, dramas, paintings, drawings, games, etc. In Botswana, one also sees youth-to-youth programs on safety and survival, covering, for example, road signs, road crossing, and first-aid techniques.

---

[1] Otaala, B. 1986. Child to child in southern Africa: a report of an international workshop held in Gaborone, Botswana, 25–29 August 1986.

In many African countries, youth-to-youth programs have developed into youth-to-community programs. In Kenya, the African Medical Relief Foundation started a pilot youth-to-youth education program in Nakuru District after people realized that the elders were going to be ineffective in health education: the health habits of the elders were already static, and the elders would not be excessively reliable in delivering health education. Initially, in 1986, the project covered 35 primary schools.

After only 3 years, a few changes were noted. First, the number of children going to clinics for the treatment of stomach upsets, parasitic infections, and similar ailments decreased by 60%, and generally the rate of pupil illness declined by 65%. Second, before the program, very few people cared about children's hygiene. Most parents left it to the teachers and vice versa. After the program was launched, parents and teachers formed voluntary groups to repair toilets and maintain cleanliness. Third, and most important, the villagers began organizing themselves to dig pit latrines for each other, at the initiative of the youth, and when the children started earning a little money making nurseries and selling seedlings, the adults also began setting up nurseries for commercial purposes (Kinunda 1989). This is one of the many examples of how the youth have contributed to community development in Africa. Although in most countries youth-to-youth and youth-to-community programs only started in the mid-1980s, they have had a big impact on communities (Howes 1988; Tay 1989). ALPID will seek to build on the excellent work of the youth in these earlier programs.

## Critical areas and needs in community development

The urban and rural poor in Africa stand a high chance of becoming even poorer if they are unable to gain access to the new ICT-driven sources of information. The causes of poverty are multiple. Africa as a continent is, in a sense, not poor, as it has a rich variety of natural resources. What is lacking are the skills to turn these resources into wealth. Therefore, at the heart of Africa's development problem is a lack of dynamic and relevant skills and the information needed to put the available skills to optimum productive use. Critical needs that ALPID can immediately address are outlined below.

### Understanding the causes of stagnation in Africa

The typical poor person in Africa is not devoid of resources, such as land or assets for use in production and distribution. Most of the poor individuals and communities in Africa lack knowledge of how to better use their natural resources, add value to their primary products, create commodities out of their materials, attract consumers from within and outside the community, etc. Most African communities, whether rural or urban, have a distance problem. Some industrial estates located in big cities are unreachable because of bad roads, personal security problems, etc. In some cases, industrial operators have had to build roads and small bridges to make their estates reachable. The rural areas are mainly accessible only by footpath and canoe. Transfer of commodities and products to and from such areas depends on human, animal, and bicycle portage. This creates a distance penalty. Anybody who wants to help reduce poverty in such areas must have a clear understanding of the role of communication infrastructure and the potential for telecommunication and information systems to reduce this distance penalty.

One also needs to see how to use existing telecommunication infrastructure to improve access to information on health, social services, environmental management, and industrial production and services. In the majority of cases, people still make only social use of telephones, where these are available. More often than not, they use telephones to reduce their need to physically go and see someone, rather than for accessing information on social services, production, distribution, or governance. ALPID will address the need for communities to change their outlook on ICTs.

## Empowering individuals and communities to help themselves

Education, health, and extension services have so far clung to classroom settings, dependent as they are on space, human resources, materials, etc. Health services have made the ill the "object," not the "subject," of health support systems. And, in industry and agriculture, extension services have had to depend on scarce extension officers, who are mostly not even eager to remain in certain areas. As the public service shrinks, moreover, it may either fail to reach the majority of producers or come to a complete standstill.

ICTs can help fill the widening gap between emerging needs and available resources. With a single, simple communication and information centre (CIC), many producers — unreached or unreachable by extension officers — can access information at a low cost. Those who cannot reach doctors for medical advice can easily access information to decide whether, when, and where to see a medical practitioner. Most important is that existing educational systems, social services, and extension support structures fail to address all the information and skills needs of various communities. CICs, if properly equipped, can provide for the needs of individuals and communities and widen their choices and opportunities.

## Managing the cultural dimensions of information domains

Communication problems in the delivery of social services, health services, and conscientization[2] programs have not received due attention. In the treatment of bilharzia, diabetes, and similar diseases, medical personnel have had immense problems getting people to bring stool or urine samples in for examination. More serious problems have surfaced in dealing with issues of sexuality and sexual behaviour. For most people, such things belong to a private information domain. Public-health information campaigns on TB and AIDS have achieved mixed results. The success of these programs depends, in many cases, on the extent to which program workers understand the divide between private and public information in African communities, particularly rural communities.

What is clear is that the private information domain is wider than the public one in many African communities. If one asks a typical African parent directly how many children he or she has, the answer may not be instantaneous. If asked how many children have died in the family, she or he may give no answer. Similarly, a typical African business person will not instantaneously answer questions about volumes of production, amounts of money, or rates of loss.

Indigenous communication packages have a lot of rites, rituals, fictions, and taboos. Communication mechanisms are songs, poems, jokes, stories, riddles, jests, etc., most of which are indirect. People using modern mass media have tried to incorporate songs, poems, and other such mechanisms into the delivery of messages, but in most cases these efforts have failed because of the mass nature of these media. In training, one should carefully ensure that information is packaged to take account of the various status systems based on age, gender, rank, title, etc. Putting women of all ages together and showing them a video may fail to convey information because this strategy fails to account for the fact that the information needs of certain groups may be private or different. Similarly, enrolling young and old people together in a class and giving them a course or showing them a video on issues of sexuality or reproductive duties and responsibilities may cause problems in many African communities.

The new ICTs carry great potential to bridge the existing information gaps. Community-based telecentres can give individuals the privacy they need to access information systems and databases. Health information systems can also be designed to help people who believe that their health is very private to access information on the symptoms of various diseases, on ways to cope with these symptoms, and on when to seek medical advice or treatment.

---

[2] An ongoing process by which a learner moves toward critical consciousness.

## Packaging and repackaging information

Africa is currently a net consumer of information packaged by other societies. Although access to such information packages may help improve productivity, we also need to package our own relevant information on indigenous systems of production and services and make it accessible to African entrepreneurs and other producers. We must develop local-area networks (LANs) and local databases on trading, manufacturing, ecology, environmental management, health facilities, etc.

We also need to disaggregate information needs by social group. Conventional mass and social media, extension services, etc., have traditionally marginalized women and their areas of specialization in agriculture, small-scale production, and trading. In rural production, most of the available information and extension support systems have focused on cash crops and livestock. They have neglected food crops and small farm animals, which are the domains of most rural women and have remained an exotic interest of some gender-conscious researchers or those doing food-security research. These areas have not had enough extension or other support. Extension officers are simply not equipped to serve such producers. Organized information databases are urgently needed to provide people in marginalized areas with information on agriculture, aquaculture, and silviculture. Retraining programs are needed for extension officers to enable them to reach out to marginalized people and focus on their activities.

In industrial production, an exchange of information on local and international markets, import and export regulations, and quality-control techniques is needed. An exchange of information would also help develop local-area trade networks on inventory and procurement systems to promote intersectoral linkages between firms of various size and specializations. ALPID will seek to build this capability, determine the relevant needs (through baseline surveys on various activities), and develop appropriate information packages to meet those needs.

## Creating an information society in Africa

Africa's indigenous information systems and networks are rapidly disappearing. Rapid urbanization and destruction of rural systems of production, coupled with the skills drain from rural to urban areas, have substantially contributed to the ossification of indigenous information systems that originally developed inside indigenous production systems and services, ecological and environmental management, and religious beliefs. Myths, rituals, rites, totems, taboos, songs, drama, art, etc., are the major means of information packaging and communication in indigenous knowledge systems. As the social, political, and ecological bases of these systems disappear, so too do the systems. ALPID will seek to build on what remains of these systems to create a wider and richer information and communication culture. ALPID will enable African communities to borrow from others to strengthen themselves as members of the global information society.

# Priority areas for intervention

To have the maximum impact, the program will concentrate on providing support in three main areas: health; small and medium-sized enterprises (SMEs); and land use and environmental management (including research on indigenous systems of production and biotechnology).

## Health

The health system in Africa is at crossroads. In the early 1970s, most countries on the continent modernized their health sectors, setting up rural and urban clinics, health centres, and even mobile clinics. African countries made medical facilities available and increased the number of hospital beds.

During the economic crisis, which became more acute in the early 1980s, these facilities began to deteriorate. Clinics were empty for lack of medicine; there were too few beds; and sterilization facilities were inadequate. Health centres began turning into death centres. In some cases, diseases such as yellow fever, cholera, leprosy, smallpox, measles, and tuberculosis, which everyone thought were on the decline, began to resurface. New deadly diseases, such as Lassa fever, Ebola, and meningitis, also began to surface, with serious consequences. Some of these diseases broke out in areas with poor sanitation and high concentrations of population, such as slums, illegal mining areas, refugee camps, and collectives.

In the background of all these developments was the return to superstition, insecurity, and fear and distrust of conventional medicine. The number of traditional healers, herbalists, and fortune-tellers increased in both rural and urban areas. Health-care delivery systems failed to adjust to these developments. Public-health programs continued to rely on "visual literacy" (Western forms of literacy), ignoring African oral traditions and systems of "audio" (informal, person-to-person) communication. Health campaigns that rely on visual literacy seem to imply a power relationship, which has made them less effective. They are seen as propaganda, owing to the assumed superiority of the demonstrator or teacher. This power relationship creates a distance between the teacher and the learner. The impact of "physical vision" (what people see and touch) in all public communications is reduced by the failure to capture "mental vision" (what people think).

In African culture, mental vision develops through personal contact. In public-health education, for example, home visits that start with greetings and conversation and end with counseling are more effective than public meetings. Oral and audio communication is very effective, both in health education and in healing, because it takes place in a narrow space; puts the learner, patient, or client at the centre; allows the learner to listen to his or her own voice and the voice of others; and permits the learner to construct, reconstruct, and deconstruct mental visions of the problem and the solution.

ALPID should build on this culture. Without playing down the importance of physical vision in health services, the program will seek to use the new ICTs to entrench the oral and audio tradition. At community telecentres, ALPID will provide information packages on sickle-cell anemia, TB, sexually transmitted diseases, HIV, hypertensive diseases, and so on. Although medicine has advanced and there are better ways of handling these diseases, information is lacking. The program will also provide information packages on dietary patterns, sanitation, hygiene, maternal and child health care, etc. Then, through home visits and other community-based interactions, the youth volunteers will attempt to change the communities' attitude toward the use, diffusion, and absorption of this health information. Once trust is established in the CICs, these centres will likely be more effective at transferring knowledge than public-health meetings are, for the following reasons:

- Public-health meetings usually occur only occasionally and take place at inconvenient times for some people. CICs will provide people with more choices and flexibility.

- Public-health meetings take a "closed-menu" approach and fail to provide enough options to solve each of the problems encountered by individuals and communities. CICs will take a "boutique" approach, with a choice of packages for individuals or groups to use whenever they prefer.

- Traditional public-health education systems take a "custodial" approach and target people in clinics who are either already ill or about to go into "medical custody." CICs will adapt a "horticultural" approach, targeting individuals and their needs whether they are ill or not.

- Conventional systems of public-health education ignore how wide the private information domain is in African culture. CICs will provide private spaces and increase and protect the private information domains of people in the community, regardless of gender, age, or status.

- CICs will build on traditional methods of healing and diagnosis, which are based on communication between humans and invisible forces, and will build on the traditional oral means of communication. These fill the gaps left by physical vision, which has failed to create effective mental vision or to reduce fear, distrust, and superstition.

To ensure compliance with medical ethics, medical specialists should accompany youth volunteers.

CICs will provide information packages on the following topics (among others):

- Common diseases and child and maternal health care;

- Dietary patterns;

- Oral health;

- Counseling for the elderly and for those who are mentally or physically disadvantaged;

- Stress, stress management, and abuse of drugs, alcohol, and other addictive substances; and

- Fertility and sex education.

To maximize the benefits of these kinds of activity, ALPID will target only closed communities, such as plantations or farming estates. Such locations have common stop shops or meeting places to use as information centres. A majority of the working people have no serious after-hours activities and could therefore spend most of their leisure time at the information centres if they found the information useful and relevant to their needs and problems.

## Small and medium-sized enterprises

In the past decade, many SMEs in Kenya, Nigeria, Tanzania, and Uganda have established subcontracting and related linkages with firms from East and Southeast Asia. These initiatives have led to significant production and technological changes. However, the SMEs still lack information on choices of suppliers for technology and technology goods, on quality control, on raw materials, on markets, etc. If they had such information, they could increase their contribution to the economic growth of the region.

SMEs, especially those in the engineering sector, have contributed substantially to the development of Africa. In some of the poorest countries on the continent, SMEs are the prime movers of industrial activity. Between 1962 and 1980, for example, Rwanda established about 220 small enterprises (GOR 1994). These have, to date, remained the most prominent feature of industrial activity in Rwanda. Mali had no industrial base in 1965, when it achieved independence. By 1985, it had 118 600 small enterprises, mostly in the rural areas (Capt 1992).

SMEs have played a significant role in poverty alleviation. But in Kenya, Nigeria, Tanzania, and Uganda, SMEs have gone beyond poverty alleviation: they have contributed substantially to employment, local skills formation, the supply of local demand, import substitution, and export promotion and have strengthened local entrepreneurship (ATP 1992; GOT 1993; Oyelaran-Oyeyinka 1996). SMEs' share of engineering-product sales averaged 21% in Tanzania and Uganda before trade liberalization and 30% after; and 10% in Kenya and Nigeria before and 15% after.

The broad categories of SMEs can be broken down into six major specializations: foundries and forges, metal fabrication, vehicle assembly and automotive components, electrical and electronic components, construction materials, and end-item assembly. SMEs operate under serious information constraints. They lack information on technology suppliers, raw-materials suppliers, markets for their products, import and export regulations, local and international demand characteristics, etc. To support the information needs of SMEs, ALPID will seek to establish the following:

- *Local-area trade networks* — Local-area databases built within LANs on production systems, order and payment procedures, volumes of production, materials, specialized products, inventory structures, etc., will be established to strengthen production management, scheduling, and quality control; to establish linkages with large-scale firms; and to reduce warehouse costs.

- *Electronic data-interchange linkages* — Links with other producers through electronic data interchanges would improve the capacity of SMEs to choose among various technology systems and suppliers and acquire new skills related to core chores, design processes, and quality-control techniques. Current links with Chinese, Korean, Malaysian, and Taiwanese firms could improve engineering capabilities.

- *Internet and e-mail links* — SMEs need online links with technology emitters such as technology laboratories, technology parks, and technology incubators (innovation laboratories); consultancy firms; advisory centres; markets; technology suppliers; and national, regional, and international research-and-development institutions.

The biggest advantage of SMEs, whether rural or urban, is that they tend to be located in the same area. To create economies of scale, they also tend to cluster themselves by specialization. Foundries and metal fabricators, for example, are likely to cluster together, which makes it easy to establish a single CIC in one industrial complex, install ICTs, and allow access at a reasonable cost.

## Land use and environmental management (including indigenous systems of production and biotechnology)

Most of the research on biotechnology has not successfully filtered into policy and production in Africa. The International Institute of Tropical Agriculture, in Nigeria, the International Livestock Research Institute, in Ethiopia and Kenya, the International Centre for Insect Physiology and Ecology, in Kenya, and the Southern African Centre for Cooperation in Agricultural and Natural Resources Research and Training, in Botswana, have all funded biotechnology research on tissue culture, embryo–ovule culture, embryo genesis, genetic improvement of tubers, gene-mapping, biofertilizers, biocides, etc. But most of the research findings have been inadequately disseminated. The same is true of most research conducted by national research institutes in Africa. Their findings need to be organized in databases.

Africa's grasslands, forests, marshes, and oceans hold precious herbs, spices, fruits, oils, resins, dyes, gums, fibres, and medicinal organisms. These resources have been wantonly harvested and exported to foreign countries for small amounts of money, and many species are now near extinction. Several nongovernmental organizations (NGOs) and research institutes have conducted research on the plunder of Africa's biodiversity, but their findings have not influenced environmental or trade policies. These findings also need to be organized in databases and made accessible to producers and policymakers. ALPID will give first priority to linking up with research institutions in environmental studies and establishing databases on available findings. It will seek to establish local-area databases and promote ICT links between researchers and policymakers.

In environmental management, the program will seek to team up with associations of small, informal-sector operators; vocational training institutions; and voluntary organizations involved in employment generation, poverty alleviation, and small-enterprise development. In collaboration with these partners, ALPID will design information packages and video and computer training programs to inculcate a culture of environmentally friendly production methods and services. It will develop databases on comparative practices, regulations, and management systems to promote awareness of import regulations pertaining to environmental standards, eco-scanning systems, and eco-labels in the management of international trade. ALPID will take the lead in developing such databases and designing training packages and materials but will not be involved in training activities.

## ALPID's target countries

The program will be implemented in four countries of sub-Saharan African (SSA): In East Africa, Kenya, Tanzania, and Uganda have been tentatively selected; in West Africa, Nigeria has been. But the list can be expanded if resources allow.

The following criteria were used in selecting and ranking the countries:

- *Telecommunications infrastructure* — The average teledensity in SSA is 0.46 lines per 100 inhabitants. With the exception of Tanzania, all the countries listed above have a reasonably high teledensity.

- *Telecommunication and information policy* — These countries either have an explicit telecommunications policy (Nigeria and Uganda) or are in the process of formulating one (Kenya and Tanzania). Most of these policies include or are likely to include guidelines on ownership and control of telecommunications; supply of Internet and e-mail services; deregulation of telecommunications-equipment, computer-hardware, and computer-software imports and of sky-based information networks; tax regimes on information and communication systems; and participation in various recently launched cable and satellite systems.

- *Good experience in youth-to-community education* — Most of these countries have had successful youth community-service programs. Kenya, Nigeria, and Tanzania have national youth service programs, which, through internship and attachment, have strengthened the integration of youth into their communities. Some of the most successful youth-to-community programs in Africa have been in the four target countries.

- *Organizational networks in the areas of health and small business* — In these four countries, the organizational infrastructure for health groups (including societies for the disabled, substance abusers, children, and the elderly), producer organizations, small-business associations, etc. is very highly developed and has been on the ground for a long time

## The process

### Target group

Youth 20–25 years old, with a college degree (or equivalent) in a discipline relevant to ALPID, will be given the opportunity to spearhead the program. ALPID will involve youth from Africa, Europe, and North America who are selected on the basis of their commitment to community development. Through training, the program will equip them with skills to use ICTs, expose them to an appropriate view of community-based development, and inculcate in them the relevant vision and values. ALPID will give these youth an opportunity to build on existing community systems of information, communication, and education to promote the acquisition, use, and diffusion of the new ICTs. Through the program, the youth will be better integrated into their communities.

## Execution of the program

ALPID will be executed in collaboration with local NGOs that have a community-based development orientation. The participating NGOs will be selected on the basis of the following criteria:

- Their experience in training youth for community development;

- Their experience in managing youth development programs;

- Their experience in managing youth-to-youth and youth-to-adult education programs; and

- Their projected budget and systems of accountability.

## Youth exchange programs

Under the program, youths from one country will have an opportunity to visit youths in other countries to share experiences. European and North American youths will get an opportunity to participate in program activities in the four countries for 3 months every year. African youths will also have an opportunity to visit information centres in Europe and North America for 1 month every year.

## Training strategies

The training program will train trainers (the youth) for 1 month, and these trainers will then train various actors in the community, upgrading these actors' information skills or enabling them to use the new ICTs. The preliminary activities of the program will include the following:

- *Selection of community-oriented youth* — ALPID will place advertisements in youth-oriented media, inviting people 20–25 years old to apply for the program. It will select 10 youths in each country and give them 1 month of intensive training and preparation at selected sites in producer, farming, and residential communities.

- *Identification of communities and institutions to link up with* — The program will identify which communities come close to its objectives and which youth would be suitable for such communities.

Table 1. Schedule of ALPID activities.

| Activities | 1997 | 1998 | 1999 | 2000 |
|---|---|---|---|---|
| 1. Selecting CBOs to work with | Dec | — | — | — |
| 2. Establishing management and administrative structure | Dec | — | — | — |
| 3. Selecting volunteers | Dec | Oct | Oct | — |
| 4. Training volunteers | — | Jan | Jan | Jan |
| 5. Deploying volunteers | — | Feb | Feb | Feb |
| 6. Assessing community needs | — | Feb | — | — |
| 7. Identifying target groups | — | Feb | — | — |
| 8. Developing LANs and developing or updating databases | — | Mar–Dec | Feb–Dec | Feb–Dec |
| 9. Experimenting with information-delivery mechanisms | — | Jul | Jul | Jul |
| 10. Training community members on the use of ICTs | — | Jul–Dec | Jul–Dec | Jul–Dec |
| 11. Setting up backup systems | — | Dec | Jan | — |
| 12. Monitoring and evaluating | — | Dec | Dec | |
| 13. Reporting | — | Jun and Dec | Jun and Dec | Jun and Dec |

Source: Based on workshop deliberations.
Note: ALPID, Youth Leadership Program for Information and Communication Technologies and Community Development in Africa; CBO, community-based organization; ICTs, information and communication technologies; LAN, local-area network.

# Activities

ALPID will carry out some of the activities outlined below, such as setting up management structures and target groups and assessing community needs, early in the project. The remaining activities will be ongoing throughout program execution (for a schedule of activities, see Table 1):

- *Setting up a management and administrative structure* — It is envisaged that the program will be implemented by an essentially pan-African youth volunteer group, although ALPID will also admit young volunteers from other countries, such as Canada, for up to 3 months. ALPID will admit, train, and assign the African volunteers to community organizations for 12 months. An overlap of intakes will allow

volunteers already in the program to train new ones for at least 1
month. The volunteers will be given a subsistence allowance and pocket
money to live and work in the communities for the period of attachment. The ALPID Secretariat will design and put into operation a management system to operationalize the program. In every country, a small
project-implementation committee will be set up to help the Secretariat
mobilize local resources and government support and to give direction.

• *Assessing community needs and identifying local resources* — Having
selected the communities, ALPID will assess their information needs,
together with their levels of communication and information literacy. It
will then identify resource persons within the communities to act as
opinion leaders or those capable of influencing the absorption of the
program. ALPID will assess local facilities and their potential to use
ICTs, as well as assessing community attitudes, knowledge, and out-
looks of traditional and new media.

• *Identifying target groups and designing information packages and databases* — Given the pluralistic nature of most of the communities in the
target countries, ALPID will have to break down groups on the basis of
their needs and levels of literacy. In the areas of health and SMEs, a
clustering of groups and subgroups will make training and the meeting
of needs easier. Data banks of environmental research will be established in close cooperation with research institutions.

• *Developing databases and LANs* — In some research organizations,
databases and LANs already exist, such as PADIS (Pan African
Documentation and Information System), AGRIS (Agricultural
Information System), and the gene bank in Arusha. The ALPID
Secretariat will ensure that the youth leadership program is linked to
these programs. Developing databases and LANs will be one of the
most tedious and demanding of activities. With the needs identified,
baseline surveys will be undertaken to establish local databases on trade
and investment patterns and on research findings that have so far been
inadequately used. The youth volunteers will have to establish their own
websites and as much as possible build in information that is relevant
to health, SMEs, and the environment. However, in all cases, efforts

will be made to tap local knowledge and build it into emerging information systems and packages.

- *Upgrading databases* — Updating the databases will be a continuous activity, calculated to keep the information current and relevant.

- *Experimenting with and selecting information-delivery mechanisms* — The nature and type of target groups will inevitably influence the choice of mechanisms and technologies to use in the various community-based information centres. Needs are not likely to be uniform, and the special needs of disabled people will also have to be taken into account. In fact, care will be taken to meet their audio and visual needs.

- *Training community members on the use of ICTs* — Activities will be launched to train the youths to use various ICTs. Some of the technologies will be visual, and some will be audio. In both cases, training on how to access information and interpret it will be crucial. The youths will have to develop an appropriate attitude toward adult education, and strict discipline will be encouraged.

- *Setting up backup systems* — To ensure continuity, ALPID will set up management, administrative, and technical backup systems.

- *Monitoring and evaluating* — The ALPID Secretariat will design mechanisms for monitoring and evaluating the program. The regular monitoring will aim at identifying the achievements and maximizing their impacts, as well as identifying obstacles and eliminating them. Capacity-building will be measured constantly, and the ALPID Secretariat will design evaluation mechanisms to adequately involve the volunteers and the communities.

## Conditions for program sustainability

A few factors will be very important to ALPID's success. Some of these are outlined below:

- *Policy support for ICTs* — Government support for the acquisition and use of ICTs will be crucial to ALPID's success. Such support would include deregulation, lower taxes on ICT imports, and permission to use public institutions, such as hospitals, community halls, and schools, to house the CICs. In some countries, the youth and the state have had very antagonistic relations, and the use of youth in community development is viewed as an obstacle. In all these cases, continuous governmental support for the program is essential.

- *Modification of attitudes and perceptions* — Many public-education officials are hooked on physical vision. This has to change to a reliance on mental vision, which can be better provided using ICTs. In addition, most people have to learn to appreciate the production value, rather than the status, of ICTs.

- *Building on community needs and strengths* — Constant needs assessment is the key to success. Information systems based on the exotic dreams of volunteers or the marketing needs of suppliers cannot remain in demand for long. The needs of the communities have to be at the centre of the program.

- *Adequate feedback mechanisms* — Regular feedback meetings will be needed to keep the interest of all stakeholders (that is, communities, community-based organizations, and relevant government departments). These meetings could be supplemented with quarterly activity reports.

- *Regular, sufficient, and timely financing* — Realistic budgets, timely financing, adequate bookkeeping, and a system of reasonably priced user charges are needed to ensure the sustainability of the CICs. A long-term objective should be to make the centres self-financing.

- *Adequate management and effective accountability* — An understanding of the problems involved in voluntary services and organizations is also essential. Management, human-resources development, and motivation strategies will be needed to keep the volunteers committed to the program and make them see themselves as part of it and to ensure that the communities do not feel like guinea pigs. Systems of accountability to the communities, actors, funders, and government bodies should be designed to ensure that the support for the program grows.

- *Equal partnership between actors and counterparts* — It is hoped that local NGOs and other organizations involved in health, youth education, and production will be very enthusiastic about teaming up with ALPID and the actors involved in the program. This enthusiasm may fade if these organizations are relegated to subsidiary roles in the process. The program should ensure that close, constant, and mutual coordination and consultation are part of its operating norms and culture. Coordinating and consultation committees should be formed in the communities and relied on to ensure that program activities conform throughout to the principles of equality and partnership.

- *Adjustment of program strategies* — Through constant monitoring and regular evaluation, the program will recognize changing needs and adjust its strategies, after consultation between the relevant actors and their program counterparts.

- *Systematic and progressive commercialization* — In the areas of SMEs and environmental research, the program should progressively design a system to commercialize access to, and use of, this information. During the second year, ALPID should carry out a market survey to determine whether the demand for information would be adequate to meet a substantial portion of the costs in the short run and all of the costs in the long run.

# References

ATP (ATP Design and Development, UK). 1992. Review of government policy as it affects small enterprises. Prepared for the Ministry of Planning and Economic Development, Government of Uganda, Kampala, Uganda.

Capt, J. 1992. Bamako and Segou (Mali). *In* Moldanado, C.; Sethuraman, S.V., ed., Technological capacity in the informal sector. International Labour Office, Geneva, Switzerland. pp. 175–199.

GOR (Government of Rwanda). 1994. Étude globale : petites et moyennes entreprises. Ministry of Finance and Economy, Kigali, Rwanda.

GOT (Government of Tanzania). 1993. Employment promotion in the informal sector: national policy for informal sector promotion. Ministry of Labour and Youth Development, Dar es Salaam, Tanzania.

Howes, H. 1988. Child to child: another path to learning. United Nations Educational, Scientific and Cultural Organization Institute for Education, Hamburg, Germany.

Kinunda, M. 1989. Kenya: health education in schools — the ECHA project. *In* Tay, A.K.B., ed., Child to child in Africa: towards an open learning strategy. United Nations Educational, Scientific and Cultural Organization; United Nations Children's Fund, Paris, France. Digest 29.

Oyelaran-Oyeyinka, B. 1996. Technology and institutions for private small and medium firms: the engineering industry in Nigeria. African Technology Policy Studies Network, Nairobi, Kenya. ATPS Research Report.

Tay, A.K.B., ed. 1989. Child to child in Africa: towards an open learning strategy. United Nations Educational, Scientific and Cultural Organization; United Nations Children's Fund, Paris, France. Digest 29.

# CHAPTER 2

# TECHNICAL FEASIBILITY OF IMPLEMENTING ALPID

*Muriuki Mureithi*

## Introduction

The Youth Leadership Program for Information and Communication Technologies and Community Development in Africa (ALPID) is an initiative of the International Development Research Centre (IDRC). The program will target small and medium-sized enterprises (SMEs) at the threshold of excellence in terms of product quality, product standards, market orientation, and export promotion. ALPID will also target rural communities with limited information sources, with a view to helping them acquire information for health, hygiene, and responsible community living. In addition, ALPID will mobilize information resources generated through local research on indigenous systems of production, biotechnology, and environment management; identify potential end-users of this information; and disseminate, popularize, and, in the long term, commercialize such information.

The main challenge for ALPID will be to improve the quality of life, production, and knowledge. Hidden within this will be smaller challenges cutting across ALPID's three priority areas. These smaller challenges will include maintaining quality in the face of rapid local, national, regional, and global change; using appropriate intervention programs; and identifying the amounts and types of resources required to put ALPID on a sustainable footing. This will have technical, technological, human, financial, and infrastructural implications. A high-quality ALPID product can only come from the input of high-quality resources. Finally, ALPID must promote and create such high quality by transforming, rather than reinforcing, the forces of alienation, or "de-Africanization."

ALPID's primary objective is to establish community-based information resources to support informed decision-making in community self-advancement and general development efforts. The program will use a youth-to-youth and youth-to-community approach to catalyze change. Skilled youth volunteers will be trained to collect and process information or identify such sources of information and establish databases of knowledge resources.

ALPID will initially provide access to information through community-based infrastructure for information and communication technologies (ICTs). This is expected to sensitize the users to the benefits of ICTs and encourage them to eventually buy their own.

With the liberalization of economies, global competition is seriously challenging the survival of SMEs. Kenyan enterprises lack the information their international competitors have to achieve efficient production. SMEs are expected to take a keen interest in ALPID and be early innovators. The target countries for the program are Kenya, Nigeria, Tanzania, and Uganda. This chapter focuses on the Kenyan situation, although it draws on comparisons with Uganda.

Preparation of this chapter involved interviews and consultations with people in various sectors, searches for available documentation on the Internet, and extensive application of my own experience.

## The Information Age and global trends[1]

A subtle transformation is now evident in the societies of developed countries. The Industrial Revolution focused attention on energy and matter, with the most visible output being tangible goods. But today, in the Information Age, intangible goods have a dominant market share. Economic output has increasingly shifted from agriculture and industry to services. In the member countries of the Organisation for Economic Co-operation and Development, the service-industry and public-sector share in the economy is now 70%, whereas manufacturing and agricultural account for only 25 and 3%, respectively (Forge 1995). This trend is also evident in the poorer countries, where the service-sector share in the economy is higher (43%) than those of manufacturing and agriculture.

This demand is creating a new industry, an industry devoted to creating, processing, and disseminating information to consumers. The information industry is now highly recognized: it creates jobs and, most important, provides important services to the entire economy. In global terms, the information industry has been growing at twice the rate of the rest of the economy. Its greatest contribution, however, will be its impacts on the efficiency and competitiveness of nations in the 21st century.

Characteristic of the emerging Information Age is the transformation of information into a commodity created, produced, manipulated, and distributed to

---

[1] This section relies on Mureithi (1997b).

consumers throughout the world. Information infrastructure is a prerequisite to participation in the Information Age.

By all parameters, target countries for ALPID fair poorly and are ill-equipped to participate in the Information Age. However, along with rural-to-urban migration, unemployment, and the immense challenges in education and health delivery, the new order also offers opportunities. Policy obstacles must be removed to foster investment in the development of information infrastructure and its applications. Countries that do have the capacity to participate in the Information Age have put in place policies to foster and promote

- Information generation, acquisition, and creation;

- Information processing, storage, and retrieval (typically, through information technologies [ITs]); and

- Information-dissemination systems (typically, through telecommunications systems).

It should be noted that as governments become more conscious of the impact of the information industry, they are putting policies in place to foster the development of ICT infrastructure and to harness its benefits and enhance development into the 21st century.

## Connectivity

Like other countries in sub-Saharan Africa (SSA), Kenya faces serious challenges in its quest to provide universal telecommunication services. By the end of July 1997, the total number of connected lines in Kenya was 269 000, generating a teledensity (ratio of telephones per 100 people in the population) of slightly less than 1%. Although this is high for SSA, which has an average teledensity of 0.5%, it is far lower than the 60% common in Europe. Yet, telecommunications applications are now available for use in health-care delivery (telemedicine, home working), telecommuting, and interactive distance learning — the very applications the country badly needs in its quest for development and newly industrialized country status by 2020. In recognition of the need to develop telecommunications, the Kenyan government published a sector policy guideline in January 1997 to chart the way forward (GOK 1997) (Figure 1).

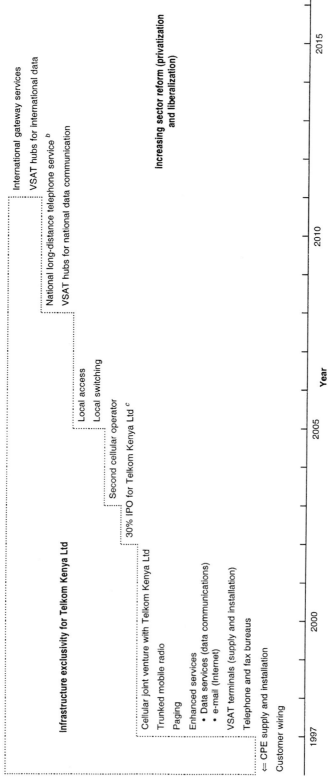

**Figure 1.** Structure of Kenya's telecommunications market. Source: Based on GOK (1997). Note: CPE, customer-premises equipment; IPO, initial public offering (of shares); VSAT, very small aperture terminal. [a] Assumed annual growth rate of 12%, based on historical performance. [b] Date of implementation subject to Ministers' discretion after evaluation of liberalization process thus far. [c] According to Nairobi Stock Exchange rules (21 Mar 1997), audited financial statements for the past 5 years (rule 5.2d) and a track record of 3 years' profitability (rule 4.3.2a) are prerequisites for a listing on the stock exchange.

Key targets were the following:

- To construct 2.7 million lines, at an estimated cost of 5.4 billion United States dollars (USD) by 2015, thereby raising national teledensity to 5% (the national teledensity spread is expected to be 20 and 1% in the urban and rural areas, respectively);

- To progressively facilitate private-sector participation in the telecommunication industry and thereby provide the bulk of the financing; and

- To unbundle the dominant player — Kenya Posts and Telecommunications Corporation (KPTC) — and establish bodies with distinct regulatory and operational mandates.

Following up on the policy paper, the government published a parliamentary bill to unbundle KPTC and establish a regulatory body and legal framework for licencing private-sector operators. At the time of writing, the bill had not been enacted by the last parliament. In line with parliamentary procedures, the bill was being redrafted for discussion in the new parliament and for enactment within the year. Kenya's telecommunication market recorded reduced investment in the last 5 years or so on account of a misunderstanding between the government and multilateral donors.

With the enactment of the bill, more opportunities for the private sector will open up, bringing fresh capital and stimulating fast growth to reduce a mounting backlog of unsatisfied customers, particularly those who want enhanced service. The public switched telecommunication network (PSTN) will continue to be a restricted domain of Telkom Kenya Ltd, the offshoot of the telecommunication component of KPTC. Regulatory provisions will continue to restrict international access to Telkom Kenya Ltd, as well as to the PSTN. The import duty for telecommunication equipment is high, raising the overall costs by 33.4% and thus affecting the affordability of services (Table 1).

KPTC manages the Kenyan telecommunication system as a monopoly. The system comprises a total switch capacity of 380 000 ports from more than 180 switches, 68% of which are digital. The 269 000 or so customers are connected through a national transmission network running on 4 400 km of terrestrial microwave (point-to-point links for telecommunications on the ground). However, international services are satellite based (Atlantic and Indian Ocean Intelsat satellites).

**Table 1.** Tariffs for ICT equipment and services, Kenya, 1997/98.

| Nomenclature | | | Rate (%) | | |
| --- | --- | --- | --- | --- | --- |
| SITC | Harmonized System | Description | Duty | VAT | Cumulative over CIF [a] |
| 8987.91.00 | 8524.99.10 | Computer discs | 15 | 16 | 33.4 |
| 8987.99.00 | 8524.99.90 | Other software | 15 | 16 | 33.4 |
|  |  | Computers | 5 | 16 | 21.8 |
| 7641.50.00 | 8517.30.00 | Telephonic or telegraphic switching apparatus | 15 | 16 | 33.4 |
| 7641.70.00 | 8517.40.00 | Other apparatus for carrier-line system | 15 | 16 | 33.4 |
| 7641.91.00 | 8517.81.00 | Telephonic | 15 | 16 | 33.4 |
| 7641.92.00 | 8517.82.00 | Telegraphic | 15 | 16 | 33.4 |
| 7643.29.00 | 8525.20.90 | Transmission apparatus incorporating reception apparatus, assembled or partly assembled | 25 | 16 | 45.0 |
| 7643.21.00 | 8525.20.10 | Unassembled | 15 | 16 | 33.4 |
| 7648.32.00 | 8526.91.00 | Radio navigational aids | 15 | 16 | 33.4 |
| 7649.10.00 | 8517.90.00 | Parts for telephone sets, video phones, cordless handsets, facsimile machines, teleprinters, and telephonic and telegraphic switching apparatus | 15 | 16 | 33.4 |
| 7649.99.00 | 8522.90.00 | Parts for any transmission apparatus other than transcribing machines, radiocassettes, dictating machines, etc. | 15 | 16 | 33.4 |
| 7649.39.00 | 8529.90.00 | Parts for use with items of SITC chapters 8525–8528 | 25 | 16 | 45.0 |
|  |  | Telephone service |  | 16 |  |
|  |  | Internet service |  | 16 |  |

Source: *The Finance Bill*, 1997.
Note: ICT, information and communication technology; SITC, Standard International Trade Classification; VAT, value-added tax.
[a] CIF, cost, insurance, and freight; calculation for indicative guidance only.

As in other public telecommunication networks in the region, the dominant product in Kenya is voice services, followed by data services; these services brought in annual revenues of about 300 million USD in 1996, making the operator the fifth largest in Africa in terms of revenue.

KPTC has implemented a packet-switching data network, with nodes in all the major towns in the country. Going under the brand name Kenpac, the network is also accessible over the PSTN. Another network, Kenstream, provides high-speed infrastructure for high-volume consumers at 64 kbps, using the existing network, with data terminal units on customers' premises. Kenstream service is only available in the main cities of Nairobi and Mombasa. Low-volume customers continue to use leased analogue circuits. With line conditioning, the PSTN can support up to 19 200 kbps. In the late 1990s, KPTC planned to launch its very small aperture terminal (VSAT) service. KPTC will restrict this service to corporate users in East African countries. With this service operational, KPTC will be able to establish communication capability in any part of the country and thereby overcome the lack of infrastructure in the rural areas.

In 1986, KPTC embarked on countrywide rural automation. It has progressively raised automation to the current level of 98%. As of 1997, only 5 500 lines were manually switched. This has generally improved the quality of service and increased the call-completion rate. Manually switched telephone exchanges are to be found in small trading centres in rural areas. This type of telephone exchange gives a reasonable quality of service for voice calls but remains problematic for data calls because of the need to manually dial a modem at the distant end. This problem has been overcome with new software. Microsoft Windows 95, for example, has a feature for manually assisted connection. Gesellschaft für Technische Zusammenarbeit (GTZ, agency for technical cooperation) is using this feature for full Internet access at two sites (three sites in Tanzania have e-mail only). The advantage of this feature is the negligible investment required to access the Internet in areas without automatic telephone service. If ALPID is implemented in an area served by a manually switched exchange, this feature will be advisable, although KPTC staff will need simple training to recognize modem calls. KPTC also uses multiaccess radio systems to provide services to widely dispersed sites. Such technology is used in large farming plantations and tourist lodges in the middle of national parks.

Since 1991 KPTC has progressively initiated measures to foster private participation in certain areas, including customer-premises equipment (CPE) – private automatic branch exchange, terminal set — telephones, and fax. The easy mode of entry into the sector and the availability of products have brought 245 companies into the CPE market, bringing tangible benefits to the consumer: lower prices, high-quality products, and support. In addition, KPTC has licenced more than 250 bureaus countrywide, and many more operate without licences, particularly in the residential areas. Paging is the only telecommunication service provided by any private-sector company.

# Developments in Uganda

In neighbouring Uganda, liberalization is happening more quickly. In January 1996, in a Telecommunication Sector Policy Announcement (TSPA), the Minister of Works, Transport and Communications promulgated the national vision for the telecommunication sector. The objective of the TSPA was to reorient sufficient private-sector capital to expand and enhance the quality of telecommunication services nationally. The government would withdraw from direct participation and actively facilitate private-sector operators as the engine of growth. The strategy to achieve this vision would be to create an enabling environment and level playing field to stimulate and build a competitive telecommunication market, with little or no intervention by the government, save that in its role as a regulator. The policy provides for the introduction of competition and licencing procedures for multiple operators and sets targets for provision of services, quality, and national spread. Key targets are the following:

- Increased network capacity — 300 000 lines in 5 years (within the same time frame, the teledensity would increase to 2 lines per 100 people from the 1996 figure of 0.25);

- Pay phones, public call offices, and other appropriate telecommunication services in the rural areas;

- Automated telephone services in all district and county headquarters; and

- A regulatory body to manage the telecommunication sector.

Uganda recently created an independent regulatory body — the Uganda Communications Commission — and awarded a licence to a private-sector PSTN operator, thus unleashing competition in all sectors of telecommunications. A mark of confidence in the growing telecommunication sector is the new network operator's commitment to pay 5.6 million USD to the government for the concession to build and operate 89 000 lines within 5 years. Although the initial target of 300 000 lines may not be realized, the network will be more advanced by far than it is today. Advertisements have appeared for the sale to the private sector of Uganda Telecom Ltd — an offshoot of the former public monopoly, Uganda Posts and Telecommunication Corporation (UPTC). With the expected completion of the process by mid-1998, Uganda will become a unique telecommunication market in the region, with full competition and the private sector playing the leading role in its development.

At the time of writing, the Uganda Communications Commission intended to establish a fund to meet the special needs of rural and disadvantaged communities and to support community-based communication initiatives, such as telecentres. One such pilot telecentre, at Nakaseke, in the famous Luwero triangle region, is supported by IDRC, the International Telecommunication Union (ITU), the United Nations Educational, Scientific and Cultural Organization, and Uganda Telecom Ltd.

# Alternative technologies

## Datacasting

Datacasting is a fast, efficient, and low-cost way to disseminate information to an unlimited number of users. Datacasting takes advantage of already existing media infrastructure, such as broadcasting — television or radio — either terrestrially or via satellite. Packet radio can also be used. Operating at higher frequencies, television may provide higher data throughput. The receiver stations have standard antennae linked to standard personal computers (PCs), with special software and hardware to receive the information. The content developer develops the data and relays these to a broadcasting company for distribution over the broadcast network. Once data are received, they are stored on the computer hard disk and can be manipulated easily to suit the user.

Typical information might be entire databases established by ALPID. A typical television "vertical blanking interval" line can transmit data at 14.4 kbps ($14\,400 \times 3\,600$ bits an hour, or 51.84 megabits of information) to many recipients simultaneously. The information can then be distributed to the target community via hard copy or any other appropriate format. This technology does not offer interactivity; however, ALPID could use it for centres in rural areas where switched telephony is unavailable. Coffee traders and paging services in Uganda are now applying variations of this technology.

## Data over radio

One commercial application of ICTs in the rural areas is the transmission of data over high-frequency radio. At transmission speeds of 2 400 bps, manuals can be sent over the system to information centres in the rural areas. ALPID can therefore use the network to disseminate data to selected centres. In Uganda, a local company, Bushnet, is providing e-mail services to rural-based organizations. Although the startup investment is up to 10 000 USD for equipment, including a computer and a monthly polling fee (and this is high for mass use), more than 40 large organizations subscribe to the network. The Ugandan government has indicated its interest in using this technology to disseminate information to rural-based departments. Although Kenyan-based intergovernmental institutions involved in relief work are using this technology, no company has offered it as a commercial service.

## Satellite

Large multinational corporations are testing global mobile personal communication systems (GMPCS), based on mobile satellite constellations orbiting the Earth. Low orbits make voice telephony possible through small handsets in any part of the world. Other services to be offered include fax, paging, and e-mail. User charges are expected to be 2–5 USD per minute, which is much higher than local PSTN tariffs. The services will therefore be aimed at international business travelers. Nevertheless, with the commercial operation of GMPCS, no point in Uganda will be without reliable communications services.

In 1998, the Iridium and Globalstar corporations were undertaking in-flight testing, with the hope of commencing commercial operations later in the year. Iridium was expected to inaugurate commercial operations on 23 September 1998, and 46 satellites of the 66-satellite constellation had already been launched and successfully tested in orbit. Two e-mail store-and-forward satellite systems can be used, Vitasat and Satellife. These operate in remote locations where terrestrial infrastructure is lacking.

The Inmarsat satellite system is already providing competitive mobile telecommunication services, using terminals the size of a laptop computer. Larger terminals are being used for more capacity, and these can be used to provide rural telephone services. Other fixed satellite systems offer telecommunication capacity, using VSATs to provide ground infrastructure. VSATs are simple to install at the point of service and are now used to provide a range of services: voice and data telecommunications, distance learning, and telemedicine. VSATs provide the best option in rural parts of Africa with no reliable telecommunication infrastructure.

## Policy and regulatory constraints

Regulatory provisions hamper the use of satellite systems in many countries. Monopoly telecommunication operators fear that VSAT and Inmarsat systems will carry telecommunication traffic away from their networks, thereby taking away revenue. In such countries, either these systems are banned or licence fees are high to dissuade people from using them, which restricts competition and maintains the high price of international telecommunication services.

All of ALPID's target countries allow the use of Inmarsat terminals and VSAT. Kenya was testing VSAT service and had approved Inmarsat in February 1998. Taxation has had a high impact on the final pricing of telecommunication products and services. In Kenya, the cumulative taxation on telecommunication equipment is 33.4%, and telecommunication services attract a value-added tax (VAT) of 16%. This has a negative impact on the affordability of these services. Governments are recognizing the role of telecommunications in national development and are looking for ways to reduce or even remove tariffs on telecommunication equipment. In December 1996, trade ministers from 32 countries, including the European Union, agreed on a timetable according to which tariffs would be completely removed by 1 January 2000 (Molony 1997). The Information Technology Agreement calls for a worldwide duty-free market for network hardware and telecommunication switching and transmission equipment. Signatories include India, Indonesia, Malaysia, and the Philippines.

The significance of the foregoing is that communication technology is available to serve ALPID in its target countries; however, regulatory and commercial issues in these communities have often hindered the use of these technologies for development. To develop telecommunication infrastructure, the target countries, especially Tanzania and Uganda, have been restructuring the sector, facilitating the input of fresh capital from the private sector, and removing barriers to accessibility by promoting competition.

## Information technology in East Africa

At the time of writing, Kenya has yet to formulate a comprehensive IT policy. Nevertheless, even without such a policy the government has taken actions with significant bearing on the development of the industry. The government has progressively reduced the tariff barriers in the IT industry, and the import duty on computers is now 5%, down from a high of 40–45% in the early 1990s. Lower duties have brought down the prices of computers and enhanced their affordability, as is evident from the increase in the number of PCs. The country has an estimated 200 000 PCs (*The East African*, 5–11 May 1997), a number expected to increase by 10–15% a year. At this level, the PC density (the number of computers per 100 people) is almost equal to teledensity at 1%. However, this compares poorly with the figures for Southeast Asian countries. By 1995, Malaysia, Singapore, and South Korea had PC densities of 3.97, 17.24, and 12.08, respectively. In the same year, South Africa had the highest PC density in Africa, at 2.65 (ITU 1996/97). Although data for Africa are largely unreliable, ITU (1996/97) estimated PC density in Nigeria at 0.41 and in Uganda at 0.05 (Table 2).

In addition to importing ITs, local entrepreneurs have established a thriving business in PC assembly. As clones of major brands, these assembled PCs come with lower price tags, which also brings pressure to bear on the prices of name-brand PCs. Similarly, a thriving local software industry is in place in Kenya, satisfying specialized needs. At least seven companies supply off-the-shelf, mass-packaged software products (Upstart Ltd Nairobi 1996). This is a major milestone in the local supply of the types of IT application needed by ALPID.

The Kenyan government has increasingly accepted the use of computers in its offices, thereby also providing a role model in the acquisition and use of ITs. The actual benefit the government offices derive from their use of ICTs is another matter, as at the time of writing the Kenyan government had no cohesive policy on the use of ITs.

As the result of the increased number of computers on the market, the sales and maintenance points have increased rapidly and spread nationally. Major towns have sales and support outlets, as well as the capacity to give training in basic computer awareness. Additionally, the government has decided to introduce computer courses in secondary schools and make the subject examinable (students must pass the course). This is going to be a major impetus for the enhancement

**Table 2.** Information-technology indicators, 1995 and 1998.

|  | Estimated PCs / 100 people, 1995 [a] | Internet hosts, Feb 1998 [b] |
|---|---|---|
| Kenya | 0.07 | 458 |
| Uganda | 0.05 | 30 |
| Tanzania | — | 25 |
| Nigeria | 0.41 | 49 |

Note: PC, personal computer.
[a] ITU (1996/97).
[b] Network Wizards (www.nw.com/zone/www/dist-bynum.html).

of IT awareness in the country. Leading the advocacy of IT development are professional IT associations, such as the Information Technology Standards Association (ITSA) and the Computer Society of Kenya. ITSA has been leading the crusade to standardize training in the industry. Continually falling prices and increased awareness of ITs will be the driving force for increased use of ITs in the coming years.

In Uganda, the environment for the IT industry is similar to that prevailing in Kenya. Uganda has no institutional framework to coordinate the orderly development of ITs. Consequently, market forces largely determine the acquisition of IT products. The import-taxation regime has not provided a sufficient margin to encourage the local assembly of equipment. Local assembly would, in time, lead to increased local content, job creation, and localization of IT products. So far, only high-income earners and institutions can afford these products. Taxation has been cited as the major factor sustaining high prices. Imported products are subject to withholding tax, import duty, and 17% VAT. These increase the end price considerably. The Internet Society of Uganda (ISUGA) has asked the government to waive taxes to make computers affordable.

Private institutions provide training, and Uganda has no local standards. Numerous companies in Kampala are offering training and appreciation courses. Nakawa Training Institute, a training school owned by UPTC, has started basic computer literacy courses and may introduce advanced courses. In light of privatization, the institute could design and implement packages for companies and for initiatives such as telecentres (Mureithi 1997a).

Finally, availability, particularly in rural areas, is restricted by problems with power, telephones, equipment sales, etc. Furthermore, companies that sell computers are largely based in Kampala and have few technical-support centres in the rural areas. Software is largely a packaged product sold by computer vendors, with little local input.

# National IT development

## Kenya

The first full Internet service was launched by the African Regional Computing Centre in the last quarter of 1995. Since then seven more Internet service providers (ISPs) have appeared. This has unleashed competition, which has brought down prices, increased the points of presence (PoP) in all major towns, and generally raised Internet awareness. The greatest challenge continues to be the low level of locally relevant information on the Internet and therefore its value. All the major towns in the country — Eldoret, Kisumu, Mombasa, and Nakuru — have an established Internet PoP in Nairobi (Box 1).

On 1 April 1997, KPTC reviewed its telephone tariff policy and enlarged the local telephone call zones to have a 60-km radius. Internet users in the environs of the PoPs therefore enjoy cheap local telephone charges. Machakos and Garissa and towns in the Mount Kenya region — Embu, Meru, and Nyeri — have to pay long-distance charges for the Internet, at 28 KES per minute (in 2000, 74.35 Kenyan shillings [KES] = 1 USD). This raises operating costs significantly. At the time of writing, KPTC's intention was to implement a national Internet backbone for as many as 30 000 customers within the year. All parts of the country are expected to be within reach of the Internet at local rates.

However, Internet development in Kenya has faced a number of constraints, especially in policy. In April 1996, KPTC declared the provision of Internet service over "privately" leased lines illegal (*The Standard*, April 1996). At the time of writing, this position had still not been publicly withdrawn. Meanwhile, African countries have been actively promoting the development of Internet use, particularly through academic institutions. A policy statement released by the Ministry of Transport and Communication in January 1997 was perhaps the first official recognition of the Internet. Currently, ISPs have to pay a hefty licence fee of 250 000 KES and a higher price for international leased lines, almost four times what ISPs have to pay in Uganda. Kenya has restricted the use of satellite technologies (that is, VSATs), which would offer cheaper international connectivity and provide more capacity than available through KPTC.

---

Box 1
**Internet service providers' websites**

- African Regional Computing Centre          www.arcc.or.ke
- Africa Online                              www.africaonline.co.ke
- Form-Net                                   www.form-net.com
- Inter-connect Connect                      www.iconnect.co.ke
- Swift Global                               www.swiftkenya.com
- Net 2000                                   www.net2000ke.com
- NairobiNet                                 www.nbnet.co.ke
- Insight Technologies                       www.insightkenya.com

Source: Summit Strategies, Nairobi, Kenya. Internal document.

Table 3. Telephone rates in Kenya, Tanzania, and Uganda, 1998.

| | Local telephone charges | | Unlimited-use charges (USD) | | Total per h (USD) |
|---|---|---|---|---|---|
| | Per min | Per h (USD) | Per month | Per h | |
| Kenya | 1.17 KES | 1.13 | 97 | 0.55 | 1.68 |
| Tanzania | 20 TZS | 1.90 | 50 | 0.28 | 2.18 |
| Uganda | 75 UGX | 4.09 | 50 | 0.28 | 4.37 |

Source: Summit Strategies, Nairobi, Kenya. Internal document.
Note: VAT not included; all Internet accounts are unlimited-use, assuming 8 hours of use in 22 days for comparison. In 2000, 74.35 Kenyan shillings (KES) = 1 United States dollar (USD); 805 Tanzanian shillings (TZS) = 1 USD; and 1520 Ugandan shillings (UGX) = 1 USD.

The higher operating charges for ISPs translate into higher charges levied to customers; consequently, Internet charges in Kenya are the highest in the region. However, extremely low local telephone rates reduce total costs (Table 3).

Moreover, governments are the largest consumers and the largest generators of information. Governments have increasingly used ICTs, particularly the Internet, to disseminate public information. The use of the Internet to disseminate public information provides a role model. Only one Internet site for the Kenyan government was found, and that was the site of the Kenyan embassy in the United States (www.embassyofkenya.com). This site had last been updated in mid-1997. There were other "national" sites, including those of the Kenya Sugar Authority (www.tcol.co.uk/orgs/ksa/kensugar.htm) and Moi University (www.tcol.co.uk/orgs/moi/moi.htm).

Government use of the Internet gives the development of ICTs a much-needed boost. The Minister of Information and Broadcasting was reported as having demanded that the Kenya Broadcasting Corporation be connected to the Internet (*The Daily Nation*, 15 February 1997). This could have a significant influence on other government departments. The private sector, in contrast, has wholeheartedly embraced ICT use. Currently, Kenya has 458 Internet hosts, the highest number in SSA outside of South Africa (see the Network Wizards website at www.nw.com/zone/www/dist-bynum.html). And Kenya has an estimated 20 000 e-mail accounts.

Although all major towns in Kenya have commercial power, large parts of the rural areas do not. Only about 7–8% of the population has access to commercial power, which also has its problems. Power failures occur often, and even when power is available, wild fluctuations occur, which are disastrous for electronic equipment. Expensive stabilizers, even generators, must be considered. This can be expected to significantly increase project costs. Some institutions have been carrying out extensive research to design cheap power solutions for ICT applications in rural areas. The South African company, BayGen, for example, manufactures simple radios that operate without batteries or other external power sources (Box 2). Apple Computers has also reportedly been researching the prospects for mass production of laptops using the cranked-radio principle. If this is successful, it will be a milestone toward a truly universal information highway traversing rural Africa.

The Kenyan government has progressively reduced import duties and VAT on photovoltaic units to promote their use and make them affordable, and the use of these units has been increasing. Kenya could be expected to sustain this policy. Eight Nairobi-based companies and numerous agents in the rural areas install and maintain the systems. More than 20 000 photovoltaic units have been sold in Kenya since 1987, largely to rural middle-class people who are integrated into the cash economy but live far from commercial power lines (World Bank 1997). Solar power is therefore a tested technology, with potential for use in ALPID projects in the rural areas. KPTC has installed solar-powered radio stations in northeastern Kenya as part of the national transmission network and has been using solar power to run small rural exchanges in areas where commercial power is unavailable. Solar energy also has the economic potential to meet energy requirements for rural communities, given the high cost of traditional network electrification.

---

Box 2

**The clockwork radio — power to the people**

The principle of the "clockwork radio" is fairly straightforward. A single winding coils the spring, much like cranking up an old gramophone. As it unwinds, the spring pushes power through a gearing mechanism to the generator. This, in turn, fuels the radio, which can run for an hour after a 25-s windup. Liberty Life, a leading South African insurance company, provided investment capital to bring the product to market in 1996, and Bay-Gen, another South African firm, is now cranking out 20 000 of the radios a month from its factory in Cape Town. Endorsed by South African President Nelson Mandela, the lunch-box-size radio is being snapped up by aid agencies such as the United Nations High Commissioner for Refugees and the International Red Cross.

Source: Barnard and Ferreira (1998).

---

Box 3
**Ugandan-government websites**

- Ugandan government                              www.uganda.co.ug
- Electoral Commission                            www.imul.com./interim
- Uganda Post Ltd                                 www.ugandaweb.com/ugapost
- Ugandan embassy in the United States            www.ugandaweb.com/ugaembassy
- Uganda Investment Authority                     www.imul.com/invest.auth/uia.html
- Makerere University                             www.imul.com/muk

Source: Summit Strategies, Nairobi, Kenya. Internal document.

---

## Uganda

The Ugandan government has embraced Internet technologies wholeheartedly, and their use has been increasing. Having several departmental websites (Box 3), the government is a role model. Many departments also have e-mail accounts.

Currently, Uganda has three major online ISPs, with close to 2 000 e-mail accounts in all. Internet accounts are fairly cheap in regional terms, facilitated by the open-sky policy adopted by the government for VSATs. Local telecommunication tariffs are, however, very high, nearly wiping out the benefit from the low cost of Internet use.

In July 1997, Uganda launched a local chapter of the Internet Society (that is, ISUGA) to act as an advocacy and sensitization group to support the development of an Internet community. At the launch of ISUGA, it was strongly felt that the government should spearhead the industry by forging a clear vision and playing a coordinating role to avoid the development of a chaotic industry. Other sensitization programs include the following.

- *The World Bank-supported School to School Initiative* — Launched in October 1996, this initiative connects three schools in Kampala to the Internet, for the development of educational activities.

- *The Uganda Connectivity Project* — Launched by a nongovernmental organization (NGO), this project promotes rural connectivity and aims at making the Internet available to the rural communities through training and the introduction of mobile "Internet centres." The project is also intended to demonstrate the use of recycled, older model computers and the feasibility of using batteries as a source of power for rural communities (Mureithi 1997a).

Despite the lack of a coordinated policy for ICT development, Uganda has no major regulatory hurdles to prevent successful implementation of ALPID. Governments still have the leeway and a duty to create a more ICT-friendly environment through lower import duties, cheaper access to international bandwidth, as in Kenya, and role modeling. In the health sector, SatelLife HealthNet Kenya pioneered the use of e-mail for health workers and provides links to critical information resources. Such efforts need to be nurtured.

# Priority areas for ALPID

## Small and medium-sized enterprises

SMEs play a dominant role in the Kenyan economy and will continue to do so in the foreseeable future. In a bid to determine the role of the SME sector, GEMINI, in conjunction with the Kenya Rural Enterprise Programme, conducted a baseline survey in 1993. A similar one was carried out in 1995, and the report, *Employment and Income in Micro and Small Enterprises in Kenya* (Daniels et al. 1995), has been widely accepted.

The report estimated that in 1995 Kenya had 708 000 enterprises employing slightly more than 1.2 million people. Urban enterprises represented 25.0% of the total and 29.1% of total created employment. Urban enterprises tended to be bigger than rural ones. The report defined microenterprises as having 10 or fewer employees and small enterprises as having 11–50. ALPID intends to focus on export-oriented enterprises in the second category, which the report found represented 0.2%, or about 1 400, of the total number of enterprises.

A survey of the industrial and technological information networks carried out by the United Nations Industrial Development Organization in 1985 revealed that the users of information included SMEs, research institutions, consultants, government policy- and decision-makers, development banks, and private individuals. Among these, the SMEs constituted the largest proportion (32.5%) (Imende 1992). The nature of the information they required varied with the nature of their business.

The Kenyan government has identified lack of information as one of the four key constraints on SME development as part of the industrialization process set out in the Republic of Kenya Session Paper No. 2 of 1996, *Industrial Transformation to the Year 2020* (ROK 1996). ALPID could significantly alleviate the information constraints in this sector.

# Intervention programs to disseminate trade information

Information is now accepted as a major trade enabler. Trade-promotion organizations rate information needs as a priority and are putting trade-information systems into their programs. All the programs recognize the value of ICTs for information processing, storage, and dissemination. In Kenya, the Export Promotion Council (EPC) is implementing a project known as the Centre for Business Information in Kenya (CEBIK), supported by the European Union. This will establish a national trade-information centre linking international and local trade-information centres. At the national level, the project will establish an inclusive relationship with other industry and trade bodies, which will consume and extend the information to their own members and generate and deliver information to CEBIK. Essentially, CEBIK intends to establish a mutually reinforcing relationship with trade-promotion and lobby organizations for the generation and consumption of trade information. Such bodies would include the Kenya Association of Manufacturers, the Kenya National Chamber of Commerce and Industry (KNCCI), the Fresh Produce Exporters Association of Kenya, and Kenya Industrial Estates.

Information requirements within the SME sector include the following (Imende 1992)

- Technical data on raw materials, finished products, and all inputs and outputs;

- Current awareness services, giving selected users information on published literature in their fields of interest and specialty;

- News bulletins, giving current information on forthcoming meetings, conferences, seminars, workshops, product exhibitions, shows, fairs, etc.;

- Standards requirements;

- Industry surveys;

- Surveys of literature on specific topics of relevance; and

- Referral, reprographic, and photographic services.

KNCCI is a nationwide organization of business people, established in 1965 as a trade and commerce advocacy and lobby group. It, too, is implementing a trade-information system. KNCCI contributes to the government's trade-policy formulation and review process. At the local level, KNCCI operates through branch offices in almost all districts. It therefore has an extensive reach in the SME sector. However, the inadequacy of its resources has been a major constraint on its impact.

A trade-information system project funded by the United Nations Development Programme has identified 10 centres across the country. These are the largest business centres at the provincial level and have fully established branch offices. Each centre will be equipped with one PC, a printer, and an Internet connection.

## Application of ICTs

The Kenyan horticultural industry is a success story, recording fast growth and claiming a leading role as exporters. In this industry, ICTs are an indispensable tool for monitoring international markets and coordinating production and harvests on the farms. This is in recognition of the competitiveness of the industry and the need for timely decision-making when dealing with perishable goods. Having used telephone and fax, the industry is now using the Internet extensively, not only for e-mail communication but also for actual sales of products! A local company, Media Street, sells flowers on the Internet and delivers them to homes in Europe within 24 h (see the Flower Highway initiative at www.eastafrica.com/flowers/ index.htm). The Kenya Agricultural Commodity Exchange is using the Internet to disseminate information on commodities and quantities of products for sale (www. arcc.or.ke/kace/cob.htm).

With the ongoing liberalization of the economy, all sectors of business are facing high competition from international competitors. Those segments of local industry with no access to information or ability to use ICTs, such as SMEs, are disadvantaged. However, large business organizations do have the ICT infrastructure, expertise, and resources to harness the technology and are increasingly using it to secure their competitive advantage.

## Intervention of ALPID

ALPID will build on EPC's and KNCCI's activities on the ground and seek to extend the information to the SME consumer while engaging this consumer as a stakeholder and generator of local information. ALPID will focus on information gathering and dissemination, using youth volunteers. To reduce the cost of infra-structure, a communal information-exchange centre should be established near the centre of SME activity.

The project will establish a comprehensive resource for local trade infor-mation. In addition, it will facilitate and provide database searches for information needed by local entrepreneurs and communication facilities. Finally, it will act as the nucleus of an electronic trade network — business people could use it to initiate trade enquiries and finalize trade deals. In the same way that leading banks install automated teller machines in supermarkets to reach the supermarket cus-tomers, trade centres, as they develop, will offer a growing and focused customer base for trade information.

## Health information for rural communities

Health care continues to pose a great challenge to Kenya. According to the devel-opment plan for 1997–2001, 60% of all diseases diagnosed in government hos-pitals are preventable. Vector-borne diseases, intestinal parasitic infections, and diarrhea are the main causes of morbidity and mortality countrywide. Preventive and promotive health initiatives would therefore have a significant impact on disease patterns. Health information is a key component in preventive health delivery.

One of the major problems facing the sector is lack of sufficient resources. Between 1980/81 and 1995/96, the annual per capita government expenditure fell from 9.82 to 6.2 USD (total allocation was estimated at 9.6% of government expenditures in the 1996/97 budget). About 80% of this expenditure has been con-centrated in the urban areas, leaving little for the rural population. Additionally, only 20% of doctors work in rural areas, but they serve 80% of the population. In 1994, the government allocated 21% of the health budget to preventive health care in rural areas. Despite the allocation of resources being skewed against the rural areas and the poor, a study cited by Plan International showed that it is 10 times more expensive to treat the same disease in a hospital than in a lower level facility. The challenge to the government, then, is to empower the lower level facilities to fight diseases and, better still, prevent their occurrence. For the latter, an empowered community is the most appropriate intervention point.

ICTs can reduce the isolation of health professionals and support the information infrastructure needed to deliver curative and preventive health ser-vices through telemedicine. Telemedicine provides access to medical services and databases via the Internet, allowing health workers to identify problems, find information on new developments, and monitor vital signs. Data on a patient's pulse rate, blood pressure, and respiratory activity, obtained with simple recording devices, can be sent to distant doctors. Teleconsultation allows image transfer and videoconferencing and consultation with local and international specialists. Tele-education provides public-care programs for health-care professionals. In the late 1990s, ITU was planning to implement pilot telemedicine programs in Tanzania and Uganda.

The ALPID target countries face serious challenges in their delivery of health services to the rural poor and would greatly benefit from telemedicine. However, the capacity of the existing telecommunication networks in these countries is inadequate for some of the advanced services mentioned above; in some cases, regulatory provisions prevent the use of a satellite with sufficient capacity.

Whereas the aspects of telemedicine discussed above largely focus on curative health delivery, ALPID will seek to empower rural communities to create local information resources for health-management information systems at the community level, using the present ICT infrastructure.

Interviews with health professionals indicated that the following types of information are needed to ensure the success of interventions through telemedicine:

- Health education to raise awareness and encourage people to change their behaviour and lifestyles;

- Health-management information to provide quantitative data for health planners;

- Technical information; and

- Information on where to get what health services.

The first obstacles to overcome are the intimidation that new technologies pose and the lack of sufficient training and incentives for staff. A project to deliver information with computers was implemented in South Africa in 1996 in Mpumalanga and Eastern Cape provinces. The project was unsuccessful because of a lack of technical support in the rural areas, and financial support eventually ceased. Health staff had a low level of computer literacy.

In a bid to increase awareness of the applications of ICTs in the health sector, HealthNet has been organizing computer-literacy courses during Health Information Week, which has been held in October every year since 1992. Another issue to address is the maintenance and support of ICT systems, particularly in rural areas, as ICT systems have high costs and low priority, especially in clinics that have problems paying for drugs and other simple requirements. The whole system needs to become sustainable and no longer dependent on donor support alone. Implementors may consider integrating the health system into the clan structure to gain support at the community level.

The use of volunteers needs careful scrutiny, as often those available turn out to be the older, unemployed, and idle ones, hoping to gain stature as a reward. Ultimately, they would have little to offer the program, and their use is now being discouraged. Consequently, whoever volunteers must be properly compensated, and ALPID has to make provisions for this.

## Entry point for ALPID

ALPID intends to establish a pilot, community-based, ICT-supported health information system, with youth volunteers providing information to the community and establishing local information resources for local health management.

The African Medical Relief Foundation (AMREF) has developed an effective and sustainable low-cost, community-based health information system applicable to rural communities in Africa (Oranga and Nordberg 1997). This system gets the community involved in planning, management, and evaluation of health programs, which in turn contributes to the sense of ownership and responsibility. Such a system generates information from the lowest level in the community (for example, the household) and is therefore more comprehensive than a facility-based system. ALPID will use ICTs to process, store, retrieve, and disseminate data to support community decision-making, with youth as the change agents.

If the community is to be a stakeholder in health issues, it must be empowered to make decisions on health management. In this context, the community will feel compelled to contribute to the financial support of the health information system. Most communities have a social infrastructure to organize social affairs, and the health needs of the community could be integrated into its plans. The NGO sector, with its population-development programs, also has a stake in the provision of health information at the community level. The sector needs detailed information to prepare proposals to access donor funds, evaluate programs, and monitor trends and variables.

## Land-use management

Information on efficient land use to increase food production and protect the environment comes to the farmer largely through extension services. The success of the extension service in Kenya can have a significant impact on its economy, considering that agriculture contributed an average 28% of Kenya's gross domestic product between 1991 and 1994. The country's strategy to industrialize by 2020 also entails heavy reliance on agricultural raw materials.

Extension services are compartmentalized into animal health, animal production, and agriculture. At the lowest administrative level, the sublocation, is the frontline extension worker (FEW). The government is the largest provider of extension services, with 80 000 staff, and is also the most broad-based in approach and application. Other providers of extension services are agricultural parastatals and boards, farmers' cooperatives, NGOs, and large industrial companies, such as Kenya Breweries, Unga Ltd, and private entrepreneurs in the agriculture business. This largely top-down approach to a passive farmer lacks coordination among the providers of extension services and therefore fails to address all the needs of the farmers. Inadequate resources seriously affect government extension services; parastatals and large companies usually focus on a single commodity such as coffee (or barley in the case of Kenya Breweries). And finally, NGOs have inadequate staying power if donor funds are withdrawn.

A new approach will empower the farmer to gradually take over extension services. This new approach will strengthen the district so that it becomes the facilitator of agricultural development, and it will strengthen the divisions so that they become service centres. Subject-matter specialists (SMS) and FEWs will be assigned to divisions. A "merry-go-round" approach will provide an intensive, time-bound (12-month) extension service to a small community of about 200 farmers.

The government has a plan to strengthen the divisions with information to empower the SMS, FEWs, and the farmer. It will set up information centres in each division. From the data available, it appears that information at the centres will be limited, considering the government will have to run more than 300 divisional information centres with limited resources; moreover, when available, the publications will be in English, thereby cutting out the large majority of people who are not proficient in this language. The government has no plans to use ICTs at the centres, and it is unlikely that the farmers will be able to collect local knowledge and store it at these centres. The government's vision is to set up an inclusive service centre for agricultural information, with the farmer as the focal point, and to harness all resources from actors in extension services.

ICTs could support and strengthen the divisional resource centres and provide a way to involve the farmer in gathering and storing indigenous farming experience and knowledge. With ICTs, the centres could integrate all extension services; strengthen farmer–researcher and farmer–extension linkages; access information from local and international sources; and create an information resource on farm and environmental resources, inputs, and markets.

## Implementation process

In all three of ALPID's priority areas, it will be imperative to sustain the project beyond its funding period. The chances of doing this would be improved by, among others things, implementing the project at lower cost; it is therefore necessary for the community to share the basic infrastructure costs where possible. Communal information bureaus have been proposed (some countries call them telecentres or telecottages). ALPID will draw on locally popular telephone bureaus but stress the use of information by and for the community. An information bureau is intended to simultaneously address issues of local connectivity, capacity-building for the target community, its lack of access to computing and communications technologies, the lack of general awareness of the potential for change, basic community development needs, etc.

KPTC has allowed and actively supported the establishment of telephone bureaus across the country. By virtue of giving customized services, these bureaus have attracted a large clientele and have been able to charge a far higher price than KPTC's coin boxes. A 3-minute local call costs 3 KES at a KPTC coin box but 10 KES at a telephone bureau. By establishing the bureaus, KPTC opened up new opportunities for entrepreneurs in the telecommunication industry. As of June 1997, KPTC had formally registered more than 250 bureaus. Many more operate without licences in residential areas. The industry is being organized by the Telecommunication Society of Kenya, a trade group established to lobby the telecommunication operator.

Similarly, ISPs have recognized the need to offer Internet services to people who do not have the basic infrastructure — PC, modem, telephone, and Internet account. Two companies, Africa Online and FormNet, have established public access points, or Internet cafés, which are gaining in popularity. As in the case of the telephone bureaus, all the Internet cafés are in the urban areas and operate commercially.

In addressing priority needs, ALPID will seek to popularize a service point offering both voice (telephony) and data (fax and Internet) communication and, more important, information to meet the specific needs of the target community. A clear will to accomplish local development objectives is a prerequisite. This includes building community awareness; offering training in the use of new technologies; incubating the development of local ICTs, businesses, and professionals; or any other objective set out by the community. The information bureaus will create a strong linkage between the target communities and ICTs and thus contribute more than the telephone bureaus, which provide only pure connectivity.

Each information bureau will have the following basic equipment in the initial phase:

- Two PCs with the appropriate software, one printer, and an uninterruptible power supply;

- At least two telephone lines, one dedicated to voice and the other to data (Internet and fax);

- An Internet connection;

- A tape recorder, a videocassette recorder (VCR), and a television set;

- Suitable accommodation, with furniture and power supply (solar power would be an option if commercial power is unavailable); and

- Transportation for the youth volunteers.

The tasks foreseen for each team require certain skills, focusing on the priority areas in ALPID. Of primary importance are the skills to operate and provide basic support for the ICTs and ICT infrastructure in the information bureaus. One key objective of the information bureaus is to incubate new ICTs in the community environment and offer simple training and support to those members of the target community who embrace ICTs and want to buy them for their own use. Also needed are the skills to design, manage, and maintain databases. Collecting data, marketing information-bureau services, and disseminating information to those who need it may require more than one youth volunteer in a team.

Efficient use of ICTs requires high-level user training, which, as noted earlier, is readily available from numerous training institutions in the country.

However, if the target communities are to use ICTs effectively, they have serious problems to overcome: language barriers, illiteracy, lack of awareness, and even lack of time to learn new skills to access information. Communities using the information bureaus should not be burdened by technology for the sake of the success of ALPID. ALPID will overcome this problem by using appropriately and well-trained youth volunteers to run the information bureaus. Each bureau will be equipped with a VCR, a television, and a tape recorder. Tape-recorded information could be viewed or heard to suit the user's capabilities. Touch-screen systems will be considered for the information bureaus, based on community needs. Essentially, ALPID will be user driven, and the technology should be transparent to the user.

ALPID will target areas of greatest impact and derive results that can be replicated in other countries. In the selection of sites for implementation, community involvement is paramount, and therefore the community must demonstrate the need for the information bureau. An information-needs assessment for the target community (in line with ALPID) will have to be carried out beforehand. Basic ICT infrastructure and maintenance support should be present. This will reduce the need to install expensive infrastructure and will enhance the bureau's integration with local ICT development. Finally, the pilot should create synergy with other government and target-community initiatives.

ALPID is expected to have a fixed time frame of 3 years, after which donor funding will cease. The project must seek and nurture partnerships with stakeholders to sustain itself. Ideally, the partners will progressively increase their share of the project burden. The information bureaus will seek to provide a service of value to the target communities, and this should be established at an early stage. The youth volunteers will be trained to gather and repackage information for the target consumers to use at their convenience. The program will make the target community aware of the information available and its potential to improve economic productivity and the quality of life. ALPID will also consider implementing a cost-sharing scheme.

# Recommendations

## Small and medium-sized enterprises

By 1995, Kenya had about 1 400 SMEs with 11–50 employees (Daniels et al. 1995). These enterprises are largely urban based. To simultaneously ensure impact and sustainability, ALPID should site its information bureaus in urban centres with a critical mass of SMEs. Nairobi has the largest number of SMEs and is therefore a recommended location.

## Health for rural communities

Between 1989 and 1993, AMREF developed and tested a community-based health information system in the Makueni District of Kenya. In the next phase, 1994–97, it implemented a pilot in the same district. Because of this project, financed by IDRC, the communities in the district (specifically, the Makindu, Kibwezi, and Mtito divisions) became fully sensitized to the need to manage their health affairs and supplement government efforts. The communities responded positively and have built nine resource centres at the sublocation level.

The project has trained volunteers to collect, analyze, and process information. Volunteers and community-based health workers, including traditional birth attendants, disseminate information through consultations and displays at the resource centres. Volunteers are civil servants, high-school leavers or graduates, health workers, and even the illiterate. All the resource centres submit information to an office at the subdistrict level in Makindu for consolidation.

A trained medical technician, provided with a PC, runs the office. An impact assessment of the project was under way at the time of writing, and preliminary results showed marked improvement in the health of the community. The government has seconded an officer to understudy the project, with a view to extending the community-based health system throughout the nation. Information from the system is used to benefit the community. For example, GTZ has used the information to monitor the growth of children under 5 years old. One constraint on the system has been in information processing. The resource centres submit information to a higher office in Makindu, but because of logistical problems it rarely comes back, and therefore the community does not benefit from the information so painstakingly collected.

ALPID should support this novel concept. It should participate in this project by strengthening resource centres in Kibwezi, Makindu, and Mtito. All the resource centres have complete physical infrastructure, commercial power, and telephones and serve a highly sensitized community. ALPID would therefore have an opportunity to exploit and demonstrate the ability of ICTs to enhance community empowerment at low cost. This project has aroused interest across the world and would therefore also give ALPID high visibility.

In other countries, the sustainability of community-based health systems is being addressed by community-based pharmacies under the framework of the Bamako Initiative. Kenya intends to implement the Bamako Initiative as well.

## Land use

The Government of Kenya has initiated a pilot program in selected districts to empower the farming community to take over land-use decision-making at the local level, under the Agricultural Sector Investment Programme. The program is to be implemented in the 1998/99 financial year, and the government is in the process of selecting the pilot districts. Of these selected districts, ALPID should focus on three that are in high-potential arid and semiarid regions.

In the meantime, the Kikuyu Division of Kiambu District is proposed for ALPID. Kikuyu Division has a high population density, which places heavy pressure on land use and may result in land degradation. The only source of livelihood in the community is small-scale farming, so the community is likely highly amenable to new approaches to enhancing land use and increasing productivity and incomes. The farming community in the area has invested modestly in information to increase productivity, and this is a basis for a sustainable ALPID program. Finally, both ICT infrastructure and commercial power are in place.

# References

Barnard, D.; Ferreira, Y. 1998. The clockwork radio — power to the people. Cited 9 Feb. e-PRODDER-mail, No. 50. Internet: www. web.co.za/prodder/

Daniels, L.; Mead, D.C.; Musinga, M. 1995. Employment and income in micro and small enterprises in Kenya: results of a 1995 survey. Kenya Rural Enterprise Programme, Nairobi, Kenya. 79 pp.

Forge, S. 1995. The consequences of current telecommunications trends for the competitiveness of developing countries. World Bank, Washington, DC, USA.

GOK (Government of Kenya). 1997. Postal and telecommunications sector policy statement. Ministry of Transport and Communications, Nairobi, Kenya. Jan 1997.

Imende, P. 1992. Information requirements and sources for small and medium scale enterprises in Kenya. Paper presented at the KIRDI Workshop on National Industrial and Technological Information Exchange and Transfer in Kenya, 25–26 Jun, Mombasa, Kenya. Kenya Industrial Research and Development Institute, Nairobi, Kenya.

ITU (International Telecommunication Union). 1996/97. World telecommunication development report. ITU, Geneva, Switzerland.

Molony, D. 1997. End-user prices to fall as import tariffs are axed. CommunicationsWeek International, 20 Jan.

Mureithi, M. 1997a. Assessment of policy options for ICT use in rural communities in Uganda. International Development Research Centre, Regional Office for Eastern and Southern Africa, Nairobi, Kenya.

———— 1997b. Building Kenya's information infrastructure for the Information Age. Information Technology Standards Association, Nairobi, Kenya.

Oranga, H.M; Nordberg, E. 1997. Community-based health information systems. African Medical Relief Foundation, Nairobi, Kenya.

ROK (Republic of Kenya). 1996. Industrial transformation to the year 2020. ROK, Nairobi, Kenya. 102 pp. Session Paper No. 2. 102 pp.

Upstart Ltd Nairobi. 1996. Micro-computer Guide, 2(4), 12–13.

World Bank. 1997. Energy sector reform and power development. World Bank, Washington, DC, USA. Project report No. 16001-Ke. 53 pp.

# Annex 1: Telecommunication infrastructure indicators

**Table A1.** Telecommunication infrastructure indicators, 1994 and 1995.

| | Socioeconomic | | Pricing (monthly subscription as % of GDP) | Teledensity (lines / 100 people) | | | Quality of service | | | |
| --- | --- | --- | --- | --- | --- | --- | --- | --- | --- | --- |
| | Population (million) | GDP per capita, 1994 | | Average | Urban [a] | Rural | Satisfied demand (%) | Waiting time for line (years) | Digitalization (%) | Faults /100 main lines |
| Kenya | 26.69 | 267 | 20.4 | 0.90 | 7.75 | 0.39 | 77.2 | 6.6 | 56.0 | 191 |
| Uganda | 19.02 | 244 | 7.5 | 0.23 | 3.47 | 0.07 | 89.6 | 1.1 | 64.2 | 80 |
| Tanzania | 29.65 | 124 | 37.7 | 0.30 | 2.19 | 0.18 | 43.3 | >10 | 42.8 | 201 |
| Nigeria | 111.27 | 412 | 6.6 | 0.36 | 1.65 | 0.34 | 80.5 | 3.5 | 42.5 | 327 |

Source: ITU (1996/97).
Note: Figures are for 1995 unless otherwise stated. GDP, gross domestic product.
[a] Refers to teledensity of the largest city.

# CHAPTER 3

# IMPLEMENTING ALPID IN KENYA: STAKEHOLDERS AND COORDINATION

*Kadzo Kogo*

## Introduction

The International Development Research Centre (IDRC), in collaboration with the African Technology Policy Studies (ATPS) network, intends to initiate a youth volunteer program: the Youth Leadership Program for Information and Communication Technologies and Community Development in Africa (ALPID). The objective of ALPID is to establish community-based information resources to support decision-making in community-based efforts for self-advancement and general development. For ALPID to achieve its objective and implement the program successfully, it must identify youth with special skills and the stakeholders with whom the youth will collaborate. This chapter identifies some of these skills and stakeholders in each of the program's three priority areas: health, production-based small and medium-sized enterprises (SMEs), and land use and environmental management.

This chapter is based on a review of secondary materials, discussions with a few people, and the consultant's long experience in community development. The review looks at issues related to the availability of skilled youth to participate in ALPID and the common social structures for disseminating information in the target communities; offers dissemination strategies; describes the various stakeholders and potential partners and their characteristics; and recommends coordination modalities for ALPID.

## Availability of skilled youth for ALPID

Since independence Kenyan government policy has been to provide access to education, especially basic education, for all Kenyans. In the past, the government invested a substantial part of its recurrent budget in education. A combination of efforts by government, nongovernmental organizations (NGOs), private schools, and individual families has given access to education to a large number of children. Kenyan society puts a high premium on educational attainment as a means to a better future and therefore makes sacrifices to ensure Kenyan children get the highest level of education.

In the 1980s, the government introduced the 8–4–4 system of education and changed the curriculum to replace the 7–6–3 system.[1] The 1979–83 development plan, whose theme was poverty alleviation, said that the purpose of changing the school curriculum was to equip graduates in rural areas with technical and vocational skills to work in agriculture, nonfarm industries, and services. At that time, the job market also had a demand for technical and vocational skills (GOK 1979).

The government also increased the number of public universities and accredited a number of private ones. Kenya now has five public universities: Nairobi, Moi, Kenyatta, Egerton, and the Jomo Kenyatta University of Agriculture and Technology. The private universities are Baraton, Daystar, the Catholic University, the United States International University in Africa, and the Methodist University. As a result, a large number of young Kenyans are obtaining college degrees each year. For example, between 1990 and 1994, the five national universities had an average enrollment of 40 116 students in their undergraduate, postgraduate, and diploma courses (CBS 1995). Kenya has, therefore, a good number of young people with degrees who are unemployed. The official figures from the Kenyan government show that 500 000 people enter the job market annually, in a country with an unemployment rate of 20%. The decline in employment in the public sector has affected university graduates, who would traditionally have been absorbed into the sector's various ministries and parastatal bodies. Graduates now have to compete for scarce jobs in the private sector or join the informal sector.

Given this state of affairs, it will be possible to recruit 20–25 year old youth with college degrees in the three ALPID focus areas. To allow for easy access and selection, the program could recruit the youth just before their graduation or through advertisements. The program could also consult some of its stakeholders and potential partners (described later in this chapter) for their advice, given their experience in development work, though not necessarily in information and communication technologies (ICTs).

---

[1] The 8–4–4 system of education has 8 years of primary school, 4 years of secondary school, and 4 years of university; and the 7–6–3 system had 7 years of primary school, 4 years of ordinary-level and 2 years of advanced-level high school, and 3 years of university (based on the British educational system).

Kenyan universities offer degrees relevant to the three focus areas. Youth with degrees in the following disciplines are therefore available in Kenya: business administration, health sciences, commerce, economics, environmental sciences, computer science, and sociology. Several commercial colleges offer computer courses in word-processing, database, spreadsheet, and statistical packages. The more reputable of the commercial colleges are Strathmore, the School of Professional Studies, and the Institute of Advanced Technology. Some of these colleges give training in e-mail and Internet use. Because of the high rate of unemployment among graduates, some youth from financially better off families attend these commercial colleges to acquire additional skills to get an advantage over others in the competition for jobs. Therefore, these colleges are also potential recruitment sources.

The recruited youth will need training in community development work, even if they hold degrees in the sectors of the ALPID focus. This is because, as will be seen later, some of the key stakeholders in the health sector are people who live and work in large plantations and farming estates, which are "closed communities"; these areas are "closed" in a real sense, as they are privately owned. Therefore, very little is known about their health and other needs or about how ICTs can be of use to them.

The community development training that ALPID's volunteers will require after recruitment is described in the following section.

## Requisite technical and social skills

In addition to having degrees in their respective disciplines, the youth volunteers should also have skills in community development so that they can work with closed communities, as some of the health data they will be collecting is of a private nature. The youth should therefore be equipped with skills to enable them to approach these communities and with the technical know-how to collect and analyze the relevant data. They should also be able to fully understand the communities' cultural and traditional practices so that they can appropriately package and disseminate the relevant information. Consequently, they will need to have the following community development skills.

### Technical skills

The youth volunteers will need research skills to collect data and compile profiles of the communities they will be working with. Community development NGOs and workers currently use rapid rural appraisal (RRA) and participatory rural appraisal (PRA) as research methods. RRA allows the researcher to rapidly get information about a small section of the population, such as a closed community. Researchers commonly use PRA when they expect to do more research and testing.

In PRA, the fundamental belief is that interventions must be designed on the basis of information generated by the people the interventions are intended to benefit. Chambers (1992) described PRA as a method of learning about rural life and conditions from, by, and with rural people. PRA can be used to identify marginalized or poor communities, services and opportunities within communities, seasonal changes, and the complexities behind people's preferences. Using this method, the youth volunteers will be able to collect information on the prevalence of diseases, production activities of SMEs, etc.

To successfully conduct PRA, the youth volunteers should also respect people's knowledge, values, and attitudes. While conducting PRA the volunteers will have an opportunity to develop a good rapport with the people in the communities. Youth volunteers will have to have the skills to develop this rapport.

## Social skills

Social skills are those the researcher or communicator uses to interact with people or to achieve a desired goal. Some of the skills needed to achieve the desired goal are the following:

- To explain concepts or ideas clearly;

- To listen well and probe to get hidden meanings in communication;

- To observe, understand, and analyze what is going on around oneself;

- To exhibit leadership in deciding on and implementing actions;

- To mobilize and motivate others to act; and

- To understand and interpret nonverbal communication.

Knowledge of group dynamics will enhance the ability of the volunteers to interact with diverse people in the communities. Generally, in a group, there are people with different characters. The volunteers should know how the positive and negative characters complement each other and when to use different characters to advantage. The volunteers should also know about behavioural patterns and how such behavioural patterns can affect the program. They should know how these behaviours can be made to complement rather than negate each other.

The youth volunteers should demonstrate leadership skills, such as respect, sensitivity to people's temperaments, and tolerance. Other leadership qualities are be an ability to listen, observe, and show respect for members of the group; honesty; and a willingness to make sacrifices for the good of the group.

By applying these skills, in combination with knowledge of the ALPID focus areas, the youth volunteers could design and package community-based information systems that will help the communities to identify resources within their own community and to use these resources to enhance their own productivity and well-being. Most Kenyan communities have a very high regard for education. They will therefore likely hold the volunteers in high esteem.

## Social structures

Most societies have structures to govern their social, productive, and religious lives. These structures aim at attaining socially meaningful goals for the members of society. The role an individual plays and the rewards reaped from playing this role are based on age, gender, power, influence, and ability. The role determines the way the individual is perceived by others in the community.

Some social structures have flexible rules governing membership, whereas others have more elaborate rules. For example, the Borana of Western Province, Kenya, have an indigenous social organization based on the principles of Peace of the Borana (known as *Nagaya Borana*) and the quality of being a Borana (known as *Bonantiti*). Their political organization is known as *gada*, a generation-based system in which one generation is assigned to maintain the Peace of the Borana. This system has rules and rituals that have been kept for centuries. The Borana also have a system of territorial organization: families are grouped into neighbourhoods, known as *solala*; neighbourhoods, into villages, called *ollaa*; villages, into *ardas*; *ardas*, into *medda*; and *meddas*, into *rela*. These territorial divisions serve as the communities' resource management units. Other less elaborate but common structures in Kenya include the following:

- *Heads of extended families* — The more cohesive extended families select a member to be their leader. People do not make important decisions regarding the family until they consult this leader, usually a man. He gives advice and resolves disputes among family members. Wealth, age, and wisdom can determine leadership in the extended family.

- *The clan* — A clan is a grouping of related extended-family members. Clan leaders, especially in Coast Province, can be very powerful. For example, they can decide how to divide the clan's land. Government workers, NGOs, and churches recognize the clan leaders as the entry points into clan-based communities.

- *Welfare societies* — Welfare societies function as support networks during emergencies. They give material and financial support when a member is bereaved; and organize and participate in cultural events, such as weddings, circumcision ceremonies, etc. Welfare associations are common in urban centres among ethnic groups from the rural areas. Some of the urban-based welfare associations are well structured, with elected officials. Besides offering support during times of need, some welfare societies invest in property, stocks, bonds, and other money-earning activities.

- *Community-based organizations* — Community-based organizations (CBOs) are groups of people who come together to pool their resources to meet a common need or goal. In areas where they are well organized and cohesive, they more or less provide the community with most of its basic services. Kenya has an estimated 30 000 CBOs.

- *Religious groups (religious societies)* — Religious groups function as welfare societies for believers. Some leaders of religious groups have a lot of power over their members, dictating social associations, modes of dress, etc.

- *Youth groups* — Youth groups can be formal or informal. Formal youth groups are the Boy Scouts, Girl Guides, Young Farmers Clubs, Wild Life Clubs, soccer clubs, and boxing clubs. Theatre, singing, counselling, and peer-education groups are some common informal groups.

- *Merry-go-rounds* — Merry-go-rounds are women-only social groups. They collect a determined amount of money, either weekly or monthly, from each group member. This money is either used to buy household utensils for members or given to a member on rotation to use as she pleases. Merry-go-rounds are usually held in members' homes or in churches.

- Nyama Choma *clubs* — *Nyama Choma* clubs are groups of people with common interests or people who work together and meet once a month to eat meat.

## Dissemination of information

In Kenya, information is disseminated in a variety of ways, both formal and informal, and the following are some examples.

### Formal information disseminators

*Barazas* are public meetings called by district officers or area chiefs to pass on information about government policies or decrees, discuss issues of public law and order, and ask the public for *harambee* money for one project or another (*harambee* are self-help initiatives in which people raise funds among themselves for a given cause). *Barazas* are also forums for professionals, in which, for example,

- Agricultural extension workers discuss the available extension services, such as improved farming methods;

- Community development assistants give people advice to improve their welfare, such as forming a women's group to start income-generating activities;

- NGO program officers inform the public of the types of project they have or would like to support in a given area; and

- Health workers usually offer information on nutrition, child care, birth planning, child health, and nutritional education and demonstrate methods for cooking the locally available food, detecting acute respiratory infection and malaria in the early stages, and preparing oral rehydration solutions.

This last point brings up a serious issue. "Often, health education messages are either inappropriate or accuse women of 'ignorance' and 'neglect'" (Eade and Williams 1995). This undermines women's positions and disempowers them, thus reducing their ability to learn. It is important to recognize the social and economic constraints that most women face and to support their efforts to deal with ill health in their communities.

### Informal information disseminators

Messages are informally relayed through the *kanga* or *lesso*, pieces of cloth used by women on the Kenyan coast. Proverbs are written on the border of the cloth. The proverbs can be either negative or positive; however, they pass on messages. People and organizations also distribute T-shirts that display certain messages.

Other informal disseminators of information are the mass media. Various organizations and the government often use the radio, television, and newspapers to widely disseminate information on health, government decrees, government propaganda, tips on motoring or gardening, etc. The Kenya Broadcasting Corporation has a weekly program, *You and Your Health*, which aims to make people aware of how to improve their health. Occasionally, the daily papers publish feature articles on SMEs or environmental issues.

Word of mouth is another way of passing on information. Community theatre has also been shown to be an effective way to communicate health information to rural communities. Comedies in the local language, containing messages of public concern, are very popular.

The youth volunteers should build on systems of informal communication already available in the communities. Then, with the members of the community and other professionals, they can develop other appropriate ways to disseminate information.

# Appropriate dissemination strategies

This section identifies appropriate dissemination strategies for ALPID in each its focus areas.

## Health

Most cultures have their own systems to explain the origin of illness. Whereas conventional science may prove that the causes of such illnesses are bacterial or viral infections, the local people may see the origin of these illnesses in social behaviour or witchcraft. It is important for ALPID to research and document the ways people use their traditional or informal health care, so that health interventions complement the original practices (at least the good ones).

If a belief in witchcraft is identified as the community's problem, the program staff should find a way to address it. One way would be for staff, with the assistance of the local leaders and the health workers in the area, to compose songs and dramas for community gatherings, such as a chief's *baraza*. One could also record or videotape these songs and dramas for use in the future. Small groups of youth, women, and men can then discuss what they have seen and heard. The Widows and Orphans Welfare Society of Kenya has used this approach in its programs in Kisumu, Nyanza Province, where people believed that HIV and AIDS were related to witchcraft.

In addition, a variety of people in the health profession, such as doctors, nurses, nutritionists, and community-based health workers, disseminate health information. However, doctors, mostly those operating private practices, concentrate mainly on curative measures; thus, people are cured but then go back to them for other ailments. The efforts of nurses and community-based health workers are constrained by lack of equipment for demonstrations and by lack of transportation, which is either unavailable or too costly. An example of a failure to emphasize preventive medicine occurred in the multisectoral Rural Development Programme of the Church of Uganda in Busoga, whose staff in the medical sector failed to include health education or other aspects of preventive medicine in the AIDS activities of their village-level health post. Similarly, the sector did little to create public awareness of HIV or AIDS, although these had been recognized as a national concern.

The mass media play a significant role in the dissemination of health information. People, especially those who have no radio or television, gather in central places (such as community centres) to listen and watch. The literate buy papers to read for themselves and pass the information on to others. However, most people have no access to radio or television, and some are illiterate and therefore cannot make use of newspapers. Using ICTs to collect and disseminate health information will be a better method to reach these people.

## Small and medium-sized enterprises

Newspapers, NGOs that carry out SME programs, and Jua Kali Associations have all greatly assisted the SME sector in Kenya. However, some SME operators lack information on markets for their products. Some do not know how to use natural materials in their production processes, perhaps because they have ignored the traditional methods of skills acquisition. The Cree of Western Bay in northern Ontario, for example, learn how to tan hides, set fishnets, and make moccasins through apprenticeships and by watching their fathers and grandfathers. Similarly, in Kenya, people once made tools such as *jembes* (hoes or forks) and *pangas* (machetes), but these skills have almost disappeared. Had these skills been retained, people in rural areas would have access to the tools they need. The Turkana of Kenya are known to be self-sufficient in the tools they need for daily life: they make knives for various purposes, cooking utensils, seats, etc. Collecting, storing, and disseminating indigenous knowledge with ICTs will help to preserve these types of skills.

## Land use and environmental management

Governments and NGOs promote the value of conserving the environment. Lesotho has a reputation of having an exceptionally eroded landscape, and many studies attribute the problem to the Basotho's "bad and primitive" land management. The government, through the state radio, ridiculed this old practice without asking the Basotho why they still held onto it. ALPID's efforts to gather and preserve indigenous knowledge will help to explain practices such as this.

## Adult-learning methods required in a youth-to-adult transfer of knowledge

To effectively transfer knowledge to adults, the youth volunteers will have to be acquainted with various methods of adult learning, such as the following:

- *Focusing on existing problems, rather than on abstract concepts; stressing "need to know" over "nice to know"; and introducing problem-solving-oriented learning* — The youth volunteers should provide skills and knowledge to use immediately to resolve real-world problems appearing on a day-to-day basis, and they should give the learners exercises to allow them to practice and apply new knowledge and skills in the educational setting before having to use them on the job. Tutorials should last no longer than 10–15 min and be followed by an opportunity for the learners to practice and apply their skills and knowledge.

- *Building on the adults' previous experience and acknowledging and incorporating the vast array of experience an adult audience brings to a learning environment* — The youth volunteers should use the adults' knowledge and experience to widen the scope of learning for other participants.

- *Providing the learners with maximum control over the learning process, based on what is needed on the job* — The instructor should be a facilitator, rather than a content specialist, and should provide options to meet individual needs and interests.

- *Teaching through active participation, involving adults in the learning process so that they learn by doing* — The youth volunteers should maximize the integration of learning by seeing, hearing, talking, and doing.

- *Using the whole–part sequencing technique* — The youth volunteers should give the "big picture," then move on to the details, and then relate the parts to the whole.

- *Using association* — The youth volunteers should focus on the adults' previous experiences, relate the new to the old, and build on known information and skills so that the learners can associate past learning with new situations.

- *Integrating holistic and analytic thinking* — Using situation analysis, for example, the youth volunteers should encourage the learners to make inductions and explore whole pictures.

- *Recognizing that adults (and, indeed, individuals of every sort) learn at different rates and in different ways* — The youth volunteers should use a variety of instructional techniques to accommodate these differences.

- *Using meaningful instructional cues and providing a clear explanation of what is to be learned, expected outcomes, and evaluation criteria* — The youth volunteers should provide the learners with tests, exercises, and cues to determine when the learners have reached competency.

- *Ensuring comprehension and retention* — The youth volunteers should check the learners' progress frequently and design activities to reinforce learning and thus to ensure comprehension and retention.

- *Providing feedback and remediation* — The youth volunteers should provide consistent information on how well the learners are progressing, give credit and recognition for success, offer remediation when errors occur, and explain why the learners were either right or wrong.

The involvement of graduates in the ALPID program will go a long way to setting role models in the communities, as these graduates will be instrumental in transferring knowledge to the adults. It is anticipated that the communities will be very receptive to the program. However, regions often have many cultural identities, and each culture may require a unique sensitivity in planning programs. Understanding cultural values is critical to any successful development program.

To achieve cultural sensitivity, the ALPID youth volunteers should familiarize themselves with the cultural practices of the target communities. They should be sensitive to people's beliefs, values, perceptions, focuses, aspirations, and hopes for self-development. It is important for the youth to take sociocultural realities into account; for example, one should know what behaviours are not allowed in groups, the ways that groups make decisions, traditional values, norms of behaviour for individuals of each gender and age group, and communication patterns. The youth should involve themselves in the communities by participating in group activities, such as discussions, communal projects, weddings, funerals, and rituals open to strangers; they should identify opinion leaders, accepted members of the community, and innovators who are likely to influence others, so as to gain acceptance and to identify with their interest group.

Such participation and involvement in the communities will help the youth establish relationships, and people will feel free to communicate information, as the youth will be assimilated into the community. Traditionally, youth respect adults, and, to some extent, adults respect educated youth. It is important that mutual trust and respect be maintained between the youth and the adults, as this will make communication easy.

The relationship between the youth volunteer and the community will have to be two-way. Communities learn from workers, and vice versa: workers should also be open and willing to learn from the communities. If the volunteer workers believe that they know everything and have the solutions to the problems and that all that the people have to do is to learn from them, then there will be no scope for any genuine dialogue between the people and the workers.

Young people are known to be energetic and dynamic. They always want to see things happening faster, whereas adults like to work at their own pace. The youth volunteer should start where the adults are and move at their pace while making it easier for them to improve their pace for quick and desirable outcomes: for sustainable development you need sensitive workers who work as partners, believe in people's potentials, and respect people's knowledge base.

Workers interested in genuine development must have faith in the people. They must believe in the people's ability to learn, analyze, act, monitor, and evaluate and bring about the desired changes. Workers show that they have faith in the people by their behaviour, their actions, and the ways they communicate. If workers have faith in people, they do not decide for them and lead them all the time, and the people are then able to take the initiative and responsibility for running their own programs and organizations.

# Key stakeholders

Each of the ALPID focus areas will have primary and secondary stakeholders. The primary stakeholders will be the communities and groups of people who use the information packages. The secondary stakeholders will be the NGOs, churches, CBOs, research institutes, universities, and government ministries that work with the communities living in the areas where the telecentres will be located. Whereas the communities, individuals, and groups will use the telecentres to access information to help them make independent decisions about their lives, the secondary stakeholders will use the telecentres to enhance their already ongoing activities, access data on which to base interventions, and decide on the best approach to use in dealing with the target communities and groups.

This section describes the primary and secondary stakeholders in each of the ALPID focus areas. Secondary stakeholders were selected from a cross-section of actors, and the list is by no means exhaustive. For example, Kenya has more than 2 000 registered NGOs, more than 23 000 women's groups, and an estimated 30 000 CBOs.

Some of the NGOs were selected because of the impact they have had on community development, vocational training, and income-generating activities and because of their technical and financial support for production-based SMEs. They were also selected because they have projects countrywide. The few CBOs were selected to illustrate how communities respond to health problems and economic deprivation. As stakeholders, their experience working with the communities will be of value to ALPID. ALPID will need to further assess some of these organizations for their suitability as program partners.

## Health

The ATPS policy paper stated that the health component of ALPID will focus on closed communities working and living in or around plantations and large farming estates. As Kenya is a mainly agricultural country, there are many large Kenyan plantations and farms growing cereals (maize, wheat, barley, etc.), temporary industrial crops (sugar cane and pyrethrum), permanent industrial crops (sisal, tea, coffee, wattle, coconut), and fruit (pineapple and cashew nuts). The government classifies plantations and farms as "large farms" if they are 700 ha or more. Such plantations and farms are mainly in Nyanza, Rift Valley, Central, Western, Coast, and Eastern provinces of Kenya (Table 1).

**Table 1.** Kenyan farms and plantations.

| | Area | | | |
|---|---|---|---|---|
| | Farms (ha) | Land (km²) | Total population | Density (people/km²) |
| Central Province | | | | |
| Kiambu | 1 568 | 2 587 | 914 412 | 353 |
| Muranga | 6 654 | 2 525 | 858 063 | 340 |
| Nyandarua | 138 | 3 373 | 345 420 | 102 |
| Nyeri | 540 | 3 266 | 607 292 | 186 |
| Eastern Province | | | | |
| Machakos | 21 336 | 13 968 | 1 402 002 | 100 |
| Nyanza Province | | | | |
| Kisii | 3 030 | 2 198 | 1 137 054 | 517 |
| Kisumu | 8 861 | 2 077 | 664 086 | 320 |
| Western Province | | | | |
| Bungoma | 6 864 | 3 072 | 679 146 | 221 |
| Kakamega | 3 782 | 3 561 | 1 463 525 | 411 |
| Coast Province | | | | |
| Kilifi | 496 | 13 006 | 91 903 | 46 |
| Kwale | 185 | 8 260 | 83 053 | 46 |
| Taita Taveta | 1 862 | 16 965 | 207 373 | 12 |
| Rift Valley Province | | | | |
| Kericho | 17 161 | 4 940 | 900 934 | 182 |
| Nandi | 20 483 | 2 784 | 433 613 | 156 |
| Laikipia | 2 810 | 9 162 | 218 957 | 24 |
| Trans Nzoia | 31 602 | 2 467 | 393 682 | 160 |
| Uasin Gishu | 57 865 | 3 218 | 445 530 | 138 |
| Nakuru | 83 648 | 7 190 | 849 096 | 118 |

Source: CBS 1986, 1994.

Plantations and farms employ a very large number of manual and factory workers. Some house their workers, whereas others rely on labour from surrounding villages. As some of the large plantations offer health services to their workers, ALPID will have to do a needs assessment to see which estates provide what types of health services.

It should be noted that these areas of Kenya show some of the worst problems of underdevelopment: high infant mortality rates; low literacy rates; large numbers of high-school dropouts; and high incidence of disease, such as typhoid, malaria, upper respiratory infection, diarrhea, and TB. The nature of the work that most people in the plantations do and their living conditions are contributing factors. One should also note that large farming estates are really closed. The landlords treat them like private property, which makes it extremely difficult to gain access to the people who work there.

Table 2 lists some secondary stakeholders that provide health services to low-income communities in Kenya.

**Table 2.** Secondary stakeholders providing health services to low-income communities in Kenya.

Africa Recovery Team

African Housing Fund

African Medical Relief Foundation

Chandaria–Minnesota International Health Volunteers and Dagoretti Community Health Services

Family Planning Association of Kenya

Kenya Aids Society

Christian Children's Fund

National Council of Churches of Kenya

Plan International

Kenya Water and Health Organisation

The Aga Khan Foundation

## Small and medium-sized enterprises

Institutions that provide vocational training in the SME sector in Kenya are listed in Table 3. The table also lists organizations that implement or support SME, employment-generation, and poverty-alleviation projects or are involved in one way or another in assisting SME production in Kenya.

**Table 3.** Secondary stakeholders providing services to SMEs in Kenya.

Vocational training in the SME sector

    Selesians of Don Bosco

    Christian Industrial Training Centres

    Strengthening Informal Sector Training and Enterprise

    The National Youth Service

    Kenya Industrial Estates

SME, employment-generation, and poverty-alleviation projects

    Kenya Rural Enterprise Programme

    Faulu Kenya

    CARE Kenya

    Nyamuyembe Complex Youth Group

    Action Aid

    Adventist Development and Relief Agency

    Pride (Kenya)

    Child Welfare Association of Kenya

    Church of the Province of Kenya

    World Vision International (Kenya)

    Kenya Community Development Trust Found

    Kenya Red Cross Society

SME production assistance

    ApproTEC ("Akili" project)

    Kisumu Innovative Centre

    Improve Your Business

    Farm Implements and Tools

    Kibuye Jua Kali Association

Note: SMEs, small and medium-sized enterprises.

**Table 4.** Secondary stakeholders involved in environmental
activities in Kenya.

African NGOs Environmental Network

Kenya Environmental Non Governmental Organisation

Mazingira Institute

Environment Liaison Centre

International Technology Development Group

Youth Programme of the United Nations Environment Programme

Tree Shade Clubs of Kenya

Wild Life Clubs of Kenya

## Environmental management and research

Table 4 lists organizations that are involved in research, networking, or support for environmental activities.

# Coordination modalities

Before the launch of ALPID, one will need to determine what coordination modalities to use. Initially, the ALPID concept will probably confuse some of the local NGOs and communities because they have not internalized the idea of ICTs as widely as other ideas, such as that of voluntarism. NGOs may also feel threatened by a project that aims to empower their "clients" to make independent decisions. Most Kenyan NGOs say they are committed to community empowerment, yet many of them disenfranchise any "beneficiaries" who dare to form alliances with rival agencies.

Kenyan CBOs, on the other hand, expect their participation to yield material gain. However, as access to ICTs will not yield "material gain" as they understand it, they might not immediately want to participate (that is, the involvement of CBOs in projects is harnessed to remuneration and not necessarily to better program delivery). Coordination with government departments, moreover, sometimes depends on the individual head of a department and the prevailing political climate. Also, although the District Development Committee is supposed to coordinate all development activities in the district, this rarely happens.

A poverty-assessment study of five districts, conducted by Matrix Development Consultants of Kenya, found that none of the towns had any organized coordination of development activities whatsoever. Some District Development Officers did not know which NGOs were in their areas or what they were doing there. As a result, there was a lot of duplication of effort. It is not unusual to find three different NGOs training community health workers in one slum area. ALPID could create opportunities for some NGOs, especially those mentioned in this chapter, to enhance their organization (and hence project capability) by establishing coordination modalities acceptable to most stakeholders.

Experience in Kenya shows that when people are consulted about new projects without being patronized, they are ready to cooperate. For example, during a program-formulation process in Migori town, an NGO consulted the entire population of potential stakeholders, seeking their views. After several meetings, a program-management committee was formed, with all stakeholders represented. What is unique about this experience is that the people in that town had never met before to discuss their common problems. The town councillors, though elected, thought they had all the answers and did not need to consult the people. Because the committee was able to consult and compromise on issues, the projects they identified as priorities were funded. ALPID could also be of service to the Kenyan government by providing data on local conditions and by training government extension workers.

Before finalizing coordination modalities, the program organizers will have to discuss the concept of ALPID with a few, but diverse, NGOs, CBOs, development departments of church organizations, and relevant government ministries to gauge their perception of the project and include their suggestions for effective programming for ALPID.

# References

CBS (Central Bureau of Statistics). 1994. Kenya population census, 1989. Volume I. CBS, Ministry of Finance and Planning, Nairobi, Kenya. 412 pp.

—— 1986. Statistical abstract, 1986. Government Printer, Nairobi, Kenya.

—— 1995. Statistical abstract, 1995. CBS, Ministry of Finance and Planning, Nairobi, Kenya.

Chambers, R. 1992. Rural appraisal: rapid, relaxed, and participatory. University of Sussex, Brighton, UK. Institute of Development Studies Discussion Paper 311.

Eade, D.; Williams, S. 1995. The Oxfam handbook of development and relief. Oxfam, Oxford, UK. 3 vols.

GOK (Government of Kenya). 1979. Fourth development plan, 1979–1983. Government Printer, Nairobi, Kenya.

CHAPTER 4

# IMPLEMENTING ALPID IN UGANDA: CHALLENGES AND POSSIBILITIES

*Agnes Katama*

## Introduction

Africa is at a crossroads. Fifteen countries in sub-Saharan Africa (SSA) have become multiparty democracies, and nearly 75% of African countries are opening up their political systems. Recent studies also suggest that policy reform and support for agricultural research are leading to rapid growth in the agricultural sector, the sector in which most African households, especially the poorest, earn a large share of their income.

Yet, the SSA nations still have the lowest levels of development in the world, as a result of formidable constraints: fragile environmental and natural-resource bases, the fastest growing populations in the world, a high incidence of AIDS and other debilitating diseases, low levels of education, extensive illiteracy, weak public institutions, poor infrastructure, and limited private sectors.

One factor differentiating the SSA nations from the developing countries of Asia and Latin America is the low level of private investment. In particular, direct foreign investment sometimes has been diverted from Africa because communications there are so difficult. A city like Manhattan has more telephone lines than all of Africa. Vast areas and low population densities make universal service expensive, and rural areas are typically negligibly served, if at all.

## The Ugandan case

Dramatic political transitions, combined with the foundations for economic and social development now in place, offer a window of opportunity for accelerating the pace of development. Nonetheless, recent accomplishments can easily be reversed if progress is not deepened and broadened.

Satisfying an acknowledged indigenous demand for information and communication technologies (ICTs) is constrained by a number of factors. Prohibitive pricing combines with other public practices and procedures to create a disabling policy environment that discourages private-sector investment in the provision of value-added ICTs. In addition, without rural telephone service more than 70% of the population is eliminated from the pool of potential users. Slow economic growth tends to further channel demand away from new technologies, which are in ant case poorly understood by local populations.

Recent World Bank economic studies have documented the correlation between information, communication, and economic growth. The economic and social utility of electronic networks is becoming more evident in a multiplicity of sectors and development endeavours. However, many factors inhibit the prolif-eration of networks in Uganda, including the poor state of the telecommunications infrastructure, lack of technical skills among personnel, poverty, and an overly restrictive regulatory framework resulting from the monopolistic production of information technology (IT) infrastructure.

How can ICTs and their development help the country? Ready access to global market information can promote broad-based, sustainable development in Africa by supporting the twin pillars of African economies: smallholder agriculture and small businesses. Improved electronic access to international investment would help African economies diversify through an expanding private sector. A growing private sector would provide off-farm employment, deepen the roles of the middle class, generate indigenous resources, and boost revenues for governments to invest in education, health, and environmental management.

## ICT development prospects

Uganda has seen a vibrant, grass-roots evolution of electronic networking during the 1990s. Sending and receiving e-mail are possible from almost every country on the continent, often through FidoNet. Information can be exchanged between FidoNet and the Internet, the de facto standard network and the backbone of grow-ing communication systems. Not one place, the Internet is, instead, a web of thousands of interconnected computer networks formed by wire, fibre optics, and even wireless links, such as radio frequencies and microwaves. Routes that sit on local networks electronically check data packets, accepting those with local addresses and forwarding those destined for other networks.

However, FidoNet uses a different protocol than the Internet. Fido is a batch-based, store-and-forward system, whereas the Internet operates in real time. As a result, Fido technology cannot offer access to the growing array of informa-tion services available on the information and communication systems of the region. Increasingly, African nations are establishing alternative connections to the

Internet. Already, a few SSA countries have public access to full Internet connectivity. Planning is under way to bring Internet connectivity to other nations in Africa, with more than 20 million United States dollars (USD) in international assistance having been made available for ICT infrastructure and training.

The sustainability of ICT investment in Africa rests on the private sector's ability to provide rural areas with Internet services and on there being a user base broad enough to make service commercially feasible. Uganda has both. Because operators have not had public subsidies for electronic communications, indigenous service providers have had to establish themselves with cost-recovery strategies in place from inception, building a solid foundation for future development.

## ICTs and the need for information

The problem of poor telecommunication infrastructure affects Uganda at every level and across every sector, from the senior policymaker to the small-scale rural farmer. The effects are so pervasive because, without reliable means of communication, Africans lack the information they need to make decisions and exercise some control over events.

In the agricultural sector, lack of information acts as a constraint on growth because it limits factor productivity. Better information about markets in other countries could lead to a larger base of demand and a higher volume of sales for individual farmers. Improved access to information could increase efficiency and productivity by enabling farmers to better plan response farming (farming choices based on trends in demand), crop choices, and inventories. At the regional level, better information and improved channels of communication could promote market integration, giving Ugandans access to a consumer pool large enough to generate economies of scale, which would enable this sector to compete internationally. In addition, better access to information from researchers and extension agents could lead farmers to adopt improved agricultural technologies and processes.

Information would play a central role in the completion of relief activities, for instance. Efforts to cost-effectively coordinate, manage, and anticipate emergency relief efforts in the country are hampered by the lack of reliable, readily accessible information on existing and potential food needs and supplies. Access to ICTs could provide a new means to improve the efficiency of relief efforts. For example, during the last few years, the World Food Programme (WFP), one of the largest movers of international food aid, has begun to electronically exchange donor food-aid delivery schedules. WFP has also begun to electronically send shipping instructions and standardized pipeline-analysis reports to concerned users. ICTs have made these developments possible.

Other knowledge-based service providers, such as teachers and medical workers, are constrained in their efforts to deliver up-to-date services to their clients because of Uganda's poor access to current research findings. The implementation of new technologies like distance learning and teleconsulting may enable knowledge workers in Uganda to overcome the constraints of their geographic isolation. By the same token, Uganda's planners, policymakers, and managers would be better able to collect or use information to improve their decision-making and, in turn, their country's ability to compete for the world's scarce resources.

The productivity of human-capital investments in Uganda is also seriously constrained by poor access to information. Researchers and scientists become isolated from current developments in their fields. Without reasonable communications, researchers lose the kind of interchange with their peers they enjoyed during their training abroad.

## The extent of information systems in Uganda

An information system comprises social structures employing various technologies to acquire, process, and disseminate information. A particular technology consists of a specific technique and the corresponding knowledge and social support required to take advantage of it.

ICTs are an important part of the enabling environment of any economy: for example, loan officers seek accurate data on rural business activities to judge the merits of business proposals; traders seek timely data on prices to know where to send buying agents; and commercial enterprises in distant towns need to hear news of tenders to keep pace with their urban competitors. All make extensive use of ITs, although perhaps not the most sophisticated ones. As there is often confusion about what ICTs actually cover, it is useful to illustrate the range of systems commonly found in Africa in general and in Uganda in particular.

Consider the system commonly used by business people of means in the fast-evolving private sector of Uganda. Sophisticated networks of commercial vehicle drivers and trusted agents visually inspect prices in remote markets and question the producers directly, then report this news to the traders (typically via mobile cellular phone), who then process the information and determine where to send their container fleets.

The traders could save time by making better use of electronic communications. A trader might use a telephone to contact a trusted colleague for remote price information. The structure of the trader's network adjusts slightly, thus obviating the need for data transmission through commercial vehicle drivers. This reduction in the number of hands through which the information must pass on its way from farm gate to trader presumably enhances its reliability, arguably improving the information system, at least from the trader's perspective.

The next step might be to have a government service in place to broadcast news of prices and supplies as observed by extension agents. This would drastically alter the nature of the information system. Traders would then rely less on their private networks of associates, but only to the extent that the public service addressed their specific needs.

The introduction of technologies to retrieve electronic information, such as Internet applications, places control of electronic information in the traders' hands, once again, and in a form with significant economies of transmission and scale. As well, libraries of information could be developed for a broad audience, queried, and selectively transmitted to traders in a useful form.

Today, Uganda already has a fairly complete range of ICTs. It is the recent introduction of Internet technologies that has attracted particular attention. Uganda is now a continental leader in advanced Internet-compatible ICTs, with a competitive market providing some of the lowest prices on the continent for access to the Internet. Only the problem of the "last mile" between service providers and information consumers constrains Uganda's further progress. This last-mile problem is more than just a result of poor telephone lines: it's also a matter of telephone penetration, which ultimately has to do with poverty.

Internet technologies are, of course, only part of what will likely be a more comprehensive information system. Which system-related technology is "more effective"? This depends entirely on the context. Other things being equal, the World Wide Web is arguably a more attractive technology than hand-carried notes. Other things rarely being equal, traders might continue to find value in an information system that relies on portable paper.

Generally, introducing the web in a setting where there are no computers, telephones, or even electricity probably makes little sense. Where computers are already in place, however, or where they are already being acquired for other purposes, the addition of Internet technologies to enhance the speed and reliability of information transmission systems is a logical next step.

A number of options would be suitable for activities where information is quite valuable or where the costs can be distributed over a large number of users.

Very small aperture terminal (VSAT) satellite systems offer the possibility of reasonably high bandwidth service (allowing more traffic along telecommunication systems, greater access to the Internet). Local Internet service providers in Kampala use VSAT systems. A satellite system installed in a remote rural town can easily provide the entire town with telephone and Internet access. Starcom, a local telecoms service provider in Uganda, for example, has introduced Internet service in Jinja. Equipment can cost as much as 100 000 USD per site, but it can serve a large number of customers. The continued feasibility of the Internet service, with retail prices set quite low by African standards, suggests that one can recover costs by distributing them over a sufficiently large number of customers (about 200 people) and make the service affordable.

Uganda is uniquely positioned to take advantage of the new technologies that marry Internet communication protocols with high-frequency radio data communications. Such groups as Bushnet and WFP have developed and used this technology. The promise is low-cost access to e-mail in remote rural locations without electricity or telephone infrastructure, and it appears that the technology delivers on this promise. The cost per site for equipment, in addition to that of a computer and electrical power supply, is about 8 000 USD. The message cost is nil. The commercial feasibility of the system is still to be documented. Should it prove to be a self-sustaining venture, it may be offered to private entrepreneurs who could offer services to users in rural locations.

An emphasis is being placed on the role of the private sector and private entrepreneurs as providers of information services. This approach is inherently sustainable from the market perspective. It is ultimately more sustainable than other approaches, such as an emphasis on project-funded service providers, because a strong and competitive local service-provider industry tends to lower unit costs. The relatively low recurring costs for information services are simply integrated into the ordinary operating expenses of the organizations that use the services, just as the costs for telephones and electricity are.

## Problems outside Kampala

Typical examples of information problems in towns outside Kampala include the following:

- Businesses fail to receive timely news of tenders offered in Kampala;

- Firms seeking capital fail to hear of visits by investors or are unavailable to present their portfolios when requests are received by agencies in Kampala;

- Banks are unable to secure timely information about funds available from central accounts in Kampala;

- Traders and other small companies are simply out of the loop for developing strategic business relationships, which are found more frequently in Kampala; and

- Project coordinators are unable to monitor activities in these towns, and their staff are unable to remain as long as they might if they were able to use e-mail to remotely manage a portion of their affairs at their Kampala offices.

# YOCO–ICT: a hypothetical coordination centre in East Africa

## Understanding the concept

The underlying principles of the Youth Leadership Program for Information and Communication Technologies and Community Development in Africa (ALPID) are appropriate for the design of a meaningful field-practice program in East Africa. Youth are idealistic, motivated, and responsive to challenges. Furthermore, as a result of fund scarcity and the need to avoid duplication of effort, ICT-based and information activities that require support must now address specific objectives on a project-by-project basis. Strategy is of the essence, and an increasingly important ingredient will be the participation of youth in the implementation and consolidation of these plans. ALPID's approach needs to match the realities within the donor agencies or funding countries, which are reluctant to finance core and administrative activities. Even though there are manifestations of donor fatigue and few tangible results, there is an appreciation within the donor community of the value added to these projects by youth.

Another important consideration is the need to apply meaningful parameters in measuring the relevance and impacts of ICT-based projects. Increasingly, donors are keen to ensure that their programs can adapt to changing dynamics on the ground and show flexibility and cost-effectiveness within the scope of their terms of reference. Coordinated assessment and evaluation mechanisms need to be revisited for the tasks at hand. Given that a growing proportion of today's civil society consists of youth, it would be most undiscerning not to include them in the design and implementation of programs that will affect their lives.

To show how ALPID might take account of these considerations, this section describes a hypothetical coordination centre in East Africa, to be run by youth undergraduates and supervised by young professionals. The centre, the Youth Community for Information and Communication Technology (YOCO–ICT), would build on existing informal networks in all university settings. Its objective would be to strengthen the operational capability of selected ICT-based setups, including securing donor goodwill as part of its general long-term commitment to strengthen the links between its target countries. Its activities should be innovative and replicable, have maximum leverage, and contribute identifiable qualitative and quantitative value added — in other words, be based on youth.

Although East Africa has taken undeniably positive steps to ensure lasting links among its ICT-based associations, it still has a need for coordination of activities at all levels. These activities should also be fundamentally unifying in character, and their success should be measurable in terms of specific collaborative initiatives in agriculture, research and development, and science and technology. Although YOCO is hypothetical, it derives from an intimate knowledge of the design and implementation of two youth projects — the University Students Attachment Programme (USAP) and the Mesh Mentoring Model Programme (Mesh Mentors, for short) — described later in this chapter.

## Funding and survival of YOCO

Tightened donor budgets notwithstanding, we have real reason to hope. When turned to constructive ends, YOCO-led initiatives or ones designed by intercountry teams would offer powerful incentives for intervention to develop meaningful strategies. A country such as Uganda has the required infrastructural base, as is evident from a recent Acacia study (Musisi 1997). However, the use of ICTs will respond to the reality on the ground. The beauty of the ALPID concept is that the natural charm and enthusiasm of youth will be enhanced by its person-to-person approach.

YOCO would need to create an ever-growing pool of expertise, resources, and experience to be a locus for the entrepreneurial spirit now characteristic of diversifying economic and investment trends in the region. The challenge is great. However, YOCO, in its commitment to see initiatives commence, would aim not only to outlive the transition but also to spearhead high-quality project development and support.

In this scenario, YOCO would be willing to act as guarantor of its own portfolio of projects and allow its growing track record of more or less successful initiatives to attract a wider partnership with donors already working with ICTs at the primary, secondary, or tertiary level. YOCO would undoubtedly draw together a body of donors, given its substantive focus on interests common to other donor-funded initiatives. The emerging body of sponsors and functional advisers would drive the building of that wider circle of associated concerns.

## Recent funding trends as a world of opportunity

To ensure the longevity of its own impact within the region and to ensure continued funding, YOCO must have a credible potential for self-sustainability and a critical mass of appeal. YOCO's activities and programs must indeed be relevant, but they must also fit into the donors' "nicheing" of funds for the region.

Ideally, YOCO would be centred in Kampala or in Dar es Salaam. Gone are the days of institution strengthening. For the longevity of this activity, it would be more appropriate to consider critical issues and provide for a centralized secretariat. The strategy would be to strike a balance between satisfying the wide array of donor concerns and achieving specific targets. The assumption is that communities in developing countries are the best judge of their own needs and excesses and their own strengths and frailties, whether this is reflected directly or by proxy. YOCO would need to pay heed to the constituencies it assisted, to re-create in itself the same "regionalization" of resources and expertise. It would provide participants with a real partnership of input and real ownership of the projects and their objectives. YOCO would help coordinate and respond to these missives.

The participatory nature of YOCO's projects points to the importance of building consensus on the applied usefulness of its activity within an accepted process of change, which would, in turn, address a critical sustainability issue. For instance, one can expect to continually witness in the next few years a considerable upsurge of gender-equity concerns voiced at all levels, with the emphasis they deserve. It is in this vein that Mesh Mentors is recommended as a possible player: in this program, girls who are preparing to enter male-dominated professions are provided with role models — young women who are already working in those professions.

YOCO's first step would be to build partnerships with parties (individuals and institutions) with parallel interests and activities. YOCO would then seek to attract the concerted and professional contribution of project designers, program leaders, and community leaders. Cooperation garnered from governments, businesses, and private voluntary agencies would be needed to build systems of innovative support that outlive the program's original mandate and spread from one country to another. YOCO would be an appropriate model for developing guidelines for collaboration.

A crucial question is whether YOCO's institutional framework would be cohesive enough to trigger, nurture, sustain, and re-create innovative models and replicate them as appropriate. ALPID's innovative approach in using youth as critical players in the design and implementation of community-based ICT projects would be an important part of the answer to this question. YOCO's evolution into an institute-like body would guarantee it the capacity to positively influence an ever-growing variety of community ICT workers. Granting an attendance certificate would make the process more academic, which would be attractive to youth and increase the program's credibility among employers, provincial administrations, and government officials, thus increasing interest in the program and support for it.

No matter what else YOCO managed to accomplish, it would need to carefully safeguard the unity of the whole while maintaining an organizational base to strengthen fledgling ICT-based initiatives and help target and follow through on various funding sources outside of the main YOCO institutional objective. A multiplicity of initiatives would thus be possible without impinging on the purity and harmony of the founding spirit of YOCO.

# Supporting youth development through professional internships — the USAP model

The skills needed to run and champion these initiatives need to be constantly enhanced. A critical and highly effective method to ensure this is systematically giving the youth on-the-job training in a real work environment. This in turn, will help the youth expand their organizational skills, time- and resource-management skills, etc. An experiment conducted over 5 years at the International Centre of Insect Physiology and Ecology (ICIPE) is a case in point. The main points are described below.

USAP is a women's empowerment project of ICIPE Science Press. The project was established in 1993 to serve the dual purpose of providing on-the-job training and reducing the number of permanent administrative staff at the press. This program takes on university students during their vacation, for a period rarely exceeding 6 months. The aims of the program are to expose students to the production of various books, journals, newsletters, brochures, etc.; and to give students an opportunity to gain work experience and learn various skills.

## Operation

USAP selects university students from various faculties who have the potential to contribute to the work at the press and places them in various departments, after intensive job training by the preceding group of "USAPers." Thereafter, the students are involved in marketing, soliciting, distribution, production liaison, mailing, and subscription activities. USAPers prepare comprehensive procedural manuals and write notes-to-file, very useful communication channels, as they smooth the flow of work. The design of USAP allows the students to work without supervision. Weekly meetings with the manager are feedback channels on tasks assigned to each person.

All USAPers can attend professional and personal development classes, which help them develop as all-round people. At the end of a full course, they are ready to give the same course to other students, or anyone else. So far, the major outlet has been to annual rural promotion projects that are normally conducted by university students. USAPers have proved to be very resourceful and often prepare the educational materials on their own, with assistance from the professionals.

## Mesh Mentors

A youth program can survive only if the ideal that forms its spine is accessible, attractive, and attainable. One such ideal is being a role model, in the sense of being a "feeling" professional. This is the thinking behind the success of Mesh Mentors as a model. This program was provoked by the need to design meaningful cocurricular activities for undergraduate women. It was generally accepted that in our public universities, women were without meaningful and substantive cocurricular activities and that undergraduate women were hard pressed to find formative activities to equip themselves with all the necessary professional skills upon graduation. One solution was to involve them centrally in the educational dynamics of high-school girls.

I have carried out considerable research regarding the feasibility of a capacitation model for women, using undergraduate or, at any rate, newly graduated women as resource persons and management trainees. Having managed a number of projects with the help of such students, I found it is possible to involve interns in a considerable number of labour-intensive initiatives, such as book fairs and rural presentations. Training is given to the girls, with the hope that they in turn will later train adolescents in communication skills, study techniques, personal hygiene, and health. An added benefit is that they relate better, given the age proximity.

In Kenya, the consortium — the Mesh Mentors — now involves more than 250 undergraduate and graduate women, at various levels of professional maturity, from all the main career areas. In Uganda, up to 154 students are involved (The Crusader 1998).

Following the Fourth World Conference on Women, it was suggested that the greatest way to empower a woman is to give her the knowledge and skills to assure herself of a significant career path. Many have stressed the need for relevant role models for women entering professional life, who, although determined to be successful, lack a point of reference and adequate moral support. The provision of role models creates meaningful communication channels, as people often emulate their senior role model. This desire to empathize is particularly strong in young people, whose natural admiration for senior role models has been the basis of the Mesh Mentors program.

This program seeks to enhance the horizontal and vertical links between professional women in influential positions and those in the making. To "mesh" is to link up in a framework that is tighter and more "commitment based" than a mere associative network. Whereas one may associate easily with one's peers at the same level (that is, horizontally), one needs a platform from which one can positively influence one's juniors (that is, vertically). Moreover, the crisscross of networked groups that the Kianda school has linked together introduces innovative ways of using university students as resource people to create more effective communication models in large institutions.

The Mesh Mentors program has been informally operational for the last 4 years (at the time of writing). Various groups are considering funding certain aspects of it. For instance, its potential to serve as an important backup for rural outreach programs for women farmers may be of interest to a nongovernmental organization for use with its own farmers in Western and Central provinces of Kenya.

## Mesh Mentoring member groups

Senior professionals coordinate and lead all the groups participating in the Mesh Mentors program. These groups are the following:

- *Women in Science* — The work of this group is to invite young girls to enter traditionally male careers in science. It has been particularly successful because the mentors are top undergraduate science students and near in age to that of the girls. This group has also injected vitality into science clubs in girls' schools, and the young women in the Women in Science group have acted as technology agents to ensure that inventions developed by the girls in these clubs reach scientific and technological practicability. Women in Science also seeks to network poorer schools with ones with better facilities, to benefit the potential scientists.

- *Women in Management, Women in Law* — Women in Management is a group of students who (with the help of professionals in the areas of economics, management, insurance, banking, capital investment, commerce, etc.) conduct basic management courses for high-school girls, give simple classes on the rudiments of bookkeeping to small-scale entrepreneurs in rural areas, and provide tuition courses for slow-learning students in poorer schools. Women in Law or law students carry out activities similar to those of their management counterparts, but with a bias toward the legal empowerment of rural women in the region. They currently provide legal advice to the other groups at the Mesh study centre.

- *Young Professionals* — The Young Professionals group comprises the working professionals who, on graduation, have benefited in some way from any of the above activities. The Young Professionals' main activities include professional mentoring of high-school girls, especially those studying technical or traditionally male-dominated subjects. The Young Professionals have considerably increased legal-rights awareness among women's entrepreneurial groups. The ever-increasing alumnae from the other groups constitute a pool of willing and dynamic youth, whose contacts and continued links with their juniors guarantee fairly high standards for the professional sessions under their care. This group is the backbone of the Mesh Mentors program, as the students in this group have worked in several outreach activities and already possess considerable organizational skills. In this group, former undergraduates, on completion of their studies, form an important resource base for ex bono mentoring and voluntary professional assistance to women of every cadre. Mesh Mentors is already a replicable model and serves young women's professional empowerment. It could also facilitate management sustainability with a format similar to that of USAP, because an important aspect of any group activity is the existing affordable, relevant, and appropriate management expertise.

# References

Crusader, The. 1998. Campus girls seek change. The Crusader, 28 Jan.

Musisi, C. 1997. Acacia Uganda strategy: technology and infrastructure options for ICTs. Paper presented at the Acacia Uganda National Strategy Workshop, 8–10 Dec, Nile International Conference Centre, Kampala, Uganda. International Development Research Centre, Ottawa, ON, Canada. 33 pp.

CHAPTER 5

# ELECTRONIC NETWORKING IN UGANDA: BUILDING LOCAL SUPPORT CAPACITY THROUGH YOUTH VOLUNTEERS

*Charles Musisi*

## Background

East Africa pioneered e-mail systems in the subregion in 1990. These systems were rudimentary, yet effective, means of communication. But they required good technical and user support. This support focused on overcoming the difficulties of using unsympathetic software and interfaces while negotiating complicated modem and terminal configurations.

Full Internet service arrived in the subregion in 1995. It was part of a technical movement that saw lower connection and equipment costs and greater processing and communications capacity. More-intuitive user interfaces have allowed easier data exchange and reduced the technical problems of linking up to service providers.

Internet protocol has introduced many benefits to users. At the same time, the burgeoning sources of information and means of delivering it have created the need for new skills. The ability to manage the retrieval, storage, and dissemination of electronic networking resources is needed for playing a brokering role for systems users.

Two means of electronic communication remain:

- Discontinuous e-mail systems, which are primarily rural and carried by FidoNet, telephone connections, and high-frequency radio links; and

- Interactive Internet systems that allow instant e-mail exchange and live browsing of the resources on the World Wide Web.

The focus of support for efficient networking is now on the following:

- New electronic information-management techniques;

- Intercommunication between discontinuous and interactive systems;

- Creation of a pool of local experience and strengthened technical capacity; and

- Solutions to the technical difficulties of extending connectivity while building self-sustaining, integrated electronic information networks.

## Makerere University

The Makerere University, Kampala (MUKLA), computer communications system has provided e-mail services within Uganda and the rest of East Africa since 1991. MUKLA was a founding member of both the East African Internet Association and the Internet Society of Uganda. It has delivered reliable links, with a global reach, to users in government, business, international agencies, community groups, and nongovernmental organizations. This experience continues with MUKLA's appropriate-technology FidoNet e-mail systems, which link rural areas that are not suited to full dial-up Internet connections. At the same time, MUKLA's role has shifted to that of an information facilitator, broker, and manager. Its new role has grown out of its experience with technical and user support for diverse sectors of Ugandan society and its economy.

## The East Africa Help Desk

The East Africa Help Desk (EAHD) was established in November 1996. It started as an initiative of the AfricaLink program, funded by the United States Agency for International Development. EAHD has helped build the capacity of networks in the countries of East Africa. Its activities include provision of technical, management, and information training and ongoing support. This support uses e-mail, telephone, and visits to user points and sites.

Staff and trainers have more than 6 years' experience in providing and servicing connectivity throughout Uganda. EAHD's clientele has expanded from development and research institutions to firms in the small-business and export sectors. The breadth of this background has given EAHD a wide base of contacts and skills to provide targeted, relevant, and effective user and networking support. Its effective time-management skills and accounting systems have ensured good business practice and maintained sustainable and successful operations.

EAHD provides the following services:

- It coordinates subregional user support and develops local networking capacities;

- It maintains Electronic Network Support Centres (ENSCs) to locate personnel and materials close to clients;

- It develops training materials and programs to provide context and instruction for electronic networking skills; and

- It trains trainers, who in turn spread technical and information proficiency on a continuous skills-transfer basis.

EAHD's target constituency is expected to extend beyond the current frontiers of AfricaLink partner networks to include other bodies promoting development. The target sectors would include education, in which training resources would unlock the information potential of global links; and small enterprises, which would gain access to new ways to reach markets and source inputs. Support would also be provided for commercial institutions seeking electronic verification and tracking of transactions through the Internet and ENSCs.

These centres extend the target areas beyond the dense capital cities and municipalities to the remote and rural regions, address the issue of the wide spatial interaction that is possible through e-mail radio links and the robust FidoNet system, and promote the integrative capacity of information management within its own technical context.

EAHD's objectives and activities are

- To respond to support calls by telephone and to offer online support by e-mail;

- To provide on-site support and training for users and information brokers;

- To sensitize management to sustainable electronic networking within their organizations;

- To maintain a remotely accessible and searchable database of frequently asked questions, support notes, and experiences;

- To initiate training and provide materials for information management and brokering;

- To provide forums for exchanging and discussing sectoral practice and activities through moderated mailing lists;

- To develop discontinuous, live, and hard-copy solutions to close gaps in information loops;

- To mobilize existing knowledge about development networking in East Africa;

- To build the capacity of information providers to develop and make local information content available;

- To forge strategic partnerships between service providers and information content providers;

- To build its own institutional capacity to meet the needs of its constituencies;

- To establish regional Networking Support and Information Centres; and

- To develop information-sharing tools and resources for common use.

Other partners or potential partners in this endeavour are the following:

- School to School Initiative (World Bank);

- Acacia Uganda Strategy, through support to secondary-school computer clubs;

- Makerere–McMaster University Partnership Program for Medical Students;

- Uganda Connectivity Project;

- MUKLA Engineering Computer Society; and

- International Association of Students in Management and Economics.

# CHAPTER 6

# IMPLEMENTING ALPID IN AFRICA: CONCLUSIONS AND RECOMMENDATIONS

*Muriuki Mureithi[1]*

## Introduction

The workshop participants were asked to suggest programs of action — within the three priority areas of land use, small and medium-sized enterprises (SMEs), and health — for the Youth Leadership Program for Information and Communication Technologies and Community Development in Africa (ALPID). This chapter outlines the implementation plans suggested by the participants.

## Land use and environmental management

The group first analyzed the issues in the land-use sector and then compartmentalized them into problem areas, using the Acacia categories of policy, infrastructure, content, and organization. ALPID's objectives in this priority area are

- To use information and communication technologies (ICTs) to improve quality of life, agricultural productivity, and incomes; and

- To ensure environmental security for farmers and peasants, as well as incorporating gender equity and sound environmental management.

The intention is that the program will make it possible to collect and popularize indigenous survival techniques, help farmers understand weather patterns and climate change, provide information on investment in crops, and measure and process outputs.

Initially, ALPID will need to analyze policies on ICTs, land use and environmental management, and youth, jointly at the regional and the national levels.

---

[1] Compiled from workshop discussions and the reports of the working groups.

This analysis should take into account the means to design information products to positively influence policy change, empower communities to effect policy reform, and enable farmers to start up their own schemes.

Policy on land use and the environment, if it is to be any good at all, must address the poor coordination of the farmer-assistance programs run by governments, nongovernmental organizations (NGOs), and others. Top-down approaches to resource management, bias against migrant farmers and women, and the subordination of indigenous knowledge need to be discouraged through the implementation of effective policy. Current policy on customary gender patterns of crop ownership and management should be examined and, if need be, changed to create an environment that does not allow gender bias in resource ownership.

In planning its infrastructure needs, ALPID should critically analyze physical facilities for telecommunications and ICT support. The target countries should have adequate energy sources to support the needed infrastructure. ICTs should have an interactive rating and may include the following:

- Datacasting, which can also be used for commercial purposes;

- Satellites (low Earth-orbiting and very small aperture terminals);

- Computers (solar powered); and

- Touch screens for ICT interfacing.

In addition, the principles of affordability and cost-effectiveness should guide ALPID's choice of ICT infrastructure; in other words, it should choose infrastructure that is easily sustainable, serviceable, and maintainable.

The ICTs should be able to provide information relevant to the needs of the communities, such as the tracking of weather and climate patterns; information on effective product management and modern methods of storage; policy-related and market information; and information on efficient production and farming systems (where to get raw materials, local prices of goods, etc.). The programs used should be easily adaptable to the communities' changing information needs and allow for networking within both local farming communities and the East African region. The main challenge for ALPID is to find ways to share essential information without intimidating the farmers.

To ensure effective programing, a needs assessment must be carried out before implementation. This will identify issues to be addressed and allow for the presentation of proposals to implement the program. In accessing information needs, program planners should use established groups, such as women's guilds and youth groups, as some of these groups have already been active in advocacy regarding the issues that ALPID seeks to address. Before the program starts, youth should be involved in internship activities in the relevant sectors, as this effort would add value to their impact in the program.

A coalition of NGOs, funding agencies, and private-sector companies should be invited to support the project. These partners would benefit from the new service and provide corporate or institutional support. Maintenance fees could be collected through user charges, which the user would pay either directly or through cooperatives, farmer associations, or government facilities.

## Small and medium-sized enterprises

Within the SME sector, firms with 1–10 employees are classified as micro-enterprises; firms with 11–50 employees, as small enterprises; and firms with 51–100 employees, as medium-sized enterprises. According to the selection criteria for this program, SMEs are defined as firms with 3–50 employees. Firms of this size will be chosen because they

- Present opportunities for enhanced indigenization within the industry;

- Have a high prospects for growth and employment;

- Have an extensive presence in rural Africa;

- Experience a severe lack of market information; and, most important,

- Make a large contribution to African industry, as they currently constitute the majority (about 70%) of continental enterprises in Africa.

Also, it was noted that larger businesses generally have their own mechanisms and resources for sourcing and synthesizing information and, as such, would not derive the same benefit from the program.

Among SMEs, the selected divisions are those of manufacturing and services, including the agroprocessing, construction, transportation, metalwork, electrical, electronics, and information technology subsectors. A lack of appropriate and readily available information has greatly inhibited these subsectors' productivity and restricted their markets.

The principle objectives of the program within the SME priority area are

- To enhance the productivity of the sector;

- To increase SMEs' access to local and international markets;

- To have a positive impact on SMEs' incomes; and

- To improve opportunities for SMEs to access international investment resources.

In addition, empowering youth with effective skills to use ICT applications and to provide information to SMEs will enable the youth to deliver the program effectively.

Successful implementation would be ensured by initially identifying the SME sector's information needs. This should be augmented by continual needs assessment and continual consolidation of an inventory of up-to-date information on SMEs. Possible sources of information are the SMEs, District Information Officers, NGOs, and community-based organizations. A wealth of information is already available, and this should be accessed and incorporated. Further, information for the SMEs should be packaged appropriately, such as in the form of flyers or databases.

The program will use sustainable technologies, especially taking into consideration the lack of electricity or infrastructural support in many rural African areas. Some appropriate and sustainable technologies have been identified:

- Land-line communication systems (telephone, fax, etc.);

- Mobile communication systems (mobile telephony, pager, etc.);

- Public switched data communication networks (Packet);

- High-frequency and very high frequency radio (datacasting), with the provision of services at low cost for rural Africa;

- Satellite systems (Inmarsat, VSAT, Domsat, Rascom, etc.);

- Mass media (newspapers, radio, and television);

- Video equipment (including playback tapes);

- Mobile cinemas;

- Computers and databases;

- Internet and e-mail;

- Intranets;

- Local-area networks; and

- Wide-area networks.

ALPID will strongly emphasize the use of simplified technologies — graphics, touch screens, and local languages (for example, Swahili, Luganda). The final choice of technology would depend on localities and content.

The choice of ICTs will depend on the centre of operation. For instance, hubs should be created to ensure access for all in major towns, whereas telecentres can be used at the provincial, district, division, and location levels. However, each of these centres should have

- Mass-media and ICT facilities, such as layout packages (PageMaker, CorelDRAW!, etc.);

- Audiovisual presentation aids, such as televisions, video, telephone, fax, and radio; and

- Access to mass-media output, such as newspapers, trade magazines, and the Internet.

Because of competition, SME's information is never broadcast and therefore many traditional delivery mechanisms, such as the chief's *baraza*, cannot be used. ALPID will emphasize technical management, information training, and support for these ICT delivery mechanisms.

Using youth as delivery agents is one of the innovations of the program. The youth should be graduates of universities or colleges, as older people, especially in the rural areas, consider these learned individuals to be young leaders.

ALPID's volunteers will undergo training for 2–3 months to gain proficiency in using ICTs, followed by hands-on deployment and participation in the exchange program. Their responsibilities would include carrying out a needs assessment and research for continuity, ensuring sustained interest in the program, and training end-users. Youth workers should receive enough remuneration to cover basic living, travel, and medical expenses. ALPID should take gender balance into consideration when recruiting the youth.

To be successful, the program should identify the major stakeholders and build strong partnerships (Table 1). The working group classified the following as the main stakeholders in this initiative: NGOs, ICT professionals and providers, SME groups and associations, governments, research institutions, sponsors, donors, youth, and telecommunication providers. ALPID's partners should have

- Proven experience in project implementation and delivery of non-financial services;

- Experience dealing with youth or volunteers and human-resource development training;

- Capabilities in project financial management;

- An intimate knowledge of local operating conditions; and

- An existing broad network of operations.

ALPID should bear in mind the differences in institutional capabilities between countries.

**Table 1.** Action plan.

| Activity | Duration (months) |
|---|---|
| Prepare a complete project document | 2 |
| Identify implementing partners in each country or region | 2 |
| Convene a workshop of stakeholders for each thematic area | 2 |

To create a conducive policy environment, the program should carry out a review of current policies and identify gaps. ALPID should then lobby the relevant authorities for changes to be made, where necessary, such as in ICT tariffs and regulations; for privatization of posts and telecommunication departments; or for expansion of easily accessible Internet services.

As program monitoring and evaluation are crucial aspects, ALPID will need to establish impact indicators, channels for feedback from end-users, and transparent accounting procedures. It should put these in place with appropriate data-capture forms and with personnel well trained in project management and problem-solving.

Sustainability could be enhanced by ensuring that SMEs begin to participate as early as possible, thus encouraging their ownership of the program. To meet program maintenance costs, ALPID should use existing infrastructure, where practical, and have a graduated fee structure for services offered. ALPID could publish and sell the information it compiles for a fee.

## Health

The program will target the following health subsectors: adolescent health and sexuality, preventive health care, and curative medicine. Common strategies for addressing these needs are the following:

- Carrying out a needs assessment (what information is needed?);

- Setting selection criteria for youth and participating communities;

- Identifying training needs;

- Developing training programs;

- Identifying key players;

- Identifying available resources;

- Establishing telecentres;

- Training peer educators; and

- Ensuring gender balance.

The program should adopt these strategies and use existing infrastructure and competencies, established health groups, and community information centres as focal points to ensure community participation.

The integration of humans and technologies should be carried out using user-friendly packages that replicate best practices. Appropriate media for the transfer of health information include

- Computers with e-mail and Internet access;

- Audiovisual equipment and radios; and

- Manuals, posters, and theatre performances.

An enabling policy environment must be in place to ensure that these activities conform to ethical and legal requirements pertaining to the use of health information or medical strategies.

The selection of sites will emphasize currently underserved locations with a high incidence of health problems, such as border and fishing communities in East Africa, where cross-community interaction is frequent. To reduce implementation costs, ALPID should find sites where it can build on existing capacities. Where possible, a regional NGO should help implement the program. The effects, successes, and failures of the program should be tracked with effective monitoring and evaluation systems, including

- Continuous assessment;

- Operational research;

- A performance-monitoring framework; and

- Tracer and baseline studies.

Youth should be involved in the program at three stages: planning, implementation, and assessment. Motivation for their involvement in the program could include a stipend of about 15 000 KES, plus travel expenses, and involvement in an exchange program with other youth volunteers (in 2000, 74.35 Kenyan shillings [KES] = 1 United States dollar [USD]). They should receive 2–3 months of training and then be deployed in the field.

Sustainability could be enhanced by promoting a government–private-sector alliance, encouraging community participation, and instituting a resource mobilization plan with cost-sharing for users. If the program is to take effect, there must be efforts to introduce the ICT into the cultural setting in which it is to be used. Also needed will be training and sensitization on the use of the technology. When selecting the youth leaders, ALPID would find it beneficial to include those from the participating communities.

# APPENDIX 1
## ACRONYMS AND ABBREVIATIONS

| | |
|---|---|
| ALPID | Youth Leadership Program for Information and Communication Technologies and Community Development in Africa |
| AMREF | African Medical Relief Foundation |
| ATPS | African Technology Policy Studies network |
| | |
| CBO | community-based organization |
| CEBIK | Centre for Business Information in Kenya |
| CIC | communication and information centre |
| CPE | customer-premises equipment |
| | |
| DHL | Document Handling Limited |
| | |
| EAHD | East Africa Help Desk [Uganda] |
| ENSC | Electronic Network Support Centre |
| EPC | Export Promotion Council [Kenya] |
| | |
| FEW | frontline extension worker |
| | |
| GDP | gross domestic product |
| GMPCS | global mobile personal communication system |
| GTZ | Gesellschaft für Technische Zusammenarbeit (agency for technical cooperation) |
| | |
| IAP | Internet access provider |
| ICIPE | International Centre of Insect Physiology and Ecology |
| ICTs | information and communication technologies |
| IDRC | International Development Research Centre |
| ISP | Internet service provider |
| ISUGA | Internet Society of Uganda |
| IT | information technology |
| ITSA | Information Technology Standards Association [Kenya] |
| ITU | International Telecommunication Union |

| | |
|---|---|
| kbps | kilobits per second |
| KES | Kenyan shilling(s) |
| KNCCI | Kenya National Chamber of Commerce and Industry |
| KPTC | Kenya Posts and Telecommunications Corporation |
| | |
| LAN | local-area network |
| | |
| MUKLA | Makerere University, Kampala [Uganda] |
| | |
| NGO | nongovernmental organization |
| | |
| PC | personal computer |
| PoP | point of presence |
| PRA | participatory rural appraisal |
| PSTN | public switched telecommunication network |
| | |
| RRA | rapid rural appraisal |
| | |
| SMEs | small and medium-sized enterprises |
| SMS | subject-matter specialist |
| SSA | sub-Saharan Africa |
| | |
| TSPA | Telecommunication Sector Policy Announcement [Uganda] |
| | |
| UPTC | Uganda Posts and Telecommunication Corporation [now Uganda Telecom Ltd] |
| USAP | University Students Attachment Programme [ICIPE Science Press] |
| USD | United States dollar(s) |
| | |
| VAT | value-added tax |
| VCR | videocassette recorder |
| VSAT | very small aperture terminal |
| | |
| WFP | World Food Programme |
| | |
| YOCO–ICT | Youth Community for Information and Communication Technology [hypothetical] |

# LIST OF WORKSHOP PARTICIPANTS

Mr Andrew O. Asibey
Co-ordinator, Evaluation
International Planned Parenthood
  Federation
Africa Regional Office
PO Box 30234
Nairobi, Kenya
Tel: 720280
Fax: 714968
E-mail: aasibey@arcc.or.ke

Mr Harun N. Baiya
Chief Executive
Strengthening Informal Sector Training and
  Enterprise
PO Box 34336
Nairobi, Kenya
Tel: 716099
Fax: 716059
E-mail: site@users.africaonline.co.ke

Mr John Baraza
Project Officer
Acacia Initiative
International Development Research Centre
Liaison House, State House Avenue
PO Box 62084
Nairobi, Kenya
Tel: 713160
Fax: 711063
E-mail: jbaraza@idrc.ca

Dr Fred Bukachi
Regional Director for Africa
Satellife HealthNet
PO Box 19387
Nairobi, Kenya
Tel: 714757
Fax: 724590
E-mail: fbukachi@ken.healthnet.org

Ms Jennifer Byarugaba
Student
Makerere University
14 Lourdel Road
PO Box 16605
Kampala, Uganda
Tel: 041-560604
Fax: 041-346730
E-mail: akatama@uol.co.ug

Mr Deogratias Fuli
Computer Systems Manager
Department of Mathematics
University of Dar es Salaam
PO Box 35062
Dar es Salaam, Tanzania
Tel: 051-410500-8 Ext. 2046
E-mail: fuli@cs.udsm.ac.tz

Mr A.R. Gacuhi
Deputy Director
Ministry of Research and Technology
PO Box 55623
Nairobi, Kenya
Tel: 216947

Mr Christophel Geerdts
Project Manager
International Development Research Centre
IDRC ROSA Mailbag
Johannesburg, South Africa
Tel: +27-11-3391911
Fax: +27-11-3395050
E-mail: idrc@wn.apc.org

Mr George Githembe
Research and Administrative Assistant
African Technology Policy Studies Network
Liaison House, State House Avenue
PO Box 62084
Nairobi, Kenya
Tel: 713160
Fax: 711063
E-mail: ggeorge@idrc.or.ke

Ms Barbara Hogan
Programme Manager
Voluntary Service Overseas
151 Slater Street, Suite 806
Ottawa, ON, Canada KIP 5H3
Tel: +1-613-234-1364
Fax: +1-613-234-1444
E-mail: barbara@vso.com

Mr Fredrick Kakaire
System Administrator
Satellife HealthNet Uganda
Medical School Mulago
PO Box 7072
Kampala, Uganda
Tel: 041-541036
Fax: 041-530024
E-mail: kakaire@uga.healthnet.org

Ms Aminah M. Kasinga
Resident Consultant
Eureka Educational and Training
    Consultants
PO Box 16746
Mombasa, Kenya
Tel: 011-221874
Fax: 011-221874

Ms Agnes Katama
Project Leader and Policy Analyst
Mesh Mentors
United Nations Development Programme
PO Box 947
Kampala, Uganda
Tel: 041-346730
E-mail: akatama@uol.co.ug

Ms Shanyisa A. Khasiani
Programme Co-ordinator and Researcher
Family Support Institute
PO Box 30913
Nairobi, Kenya
Tel: 226350
Fax: 251107

Ms Mwihaki Kimura
Co-ordinator
Ungana – Young Friends of AMREF
Wilson Airport
PO Box 30125
Nairobi, Kenya
Tel: 501301
Fax: 606345
E-mail: ungana@swiftkenya.com

Ms Kadzo Kogo
Associate Director
Development Associates
PO Box 61381
Nairobi, Kenya
Tel: 500033
Fax: 500033

Dr Yadon Mtarima Kohi
Director General
Tanzania Commission for Science and
    Technology
Ali Hassan Mwinyi Road
PO Box 4302
Dar es Salaam, Tanzania
Tel: 051-700750
Fax: 051-75313
E-mail: costech@costech.gn.apc.org

Dr Davinder Lamba
Executive Director
Mazingira Institute
PO Box 14550
Nairobi, Kenya
Tel: 443219
Fax: 444643
E-mail: mazingira@elci.sasa.unep.no

Mr Barney Lodge
Managing Director
Media Street Limited
Longonot Place, Kijabe Street
PO Box 24262
Nairobi, Kenya
Tel: 210217
Fax: 220158
E-mail: barney@eastafrica.com

Ms Aileen Lyon
Programme Director
Volunteer Service Overseas
Ngong Road
PO Box 56413
Nairobi, Kenya
Tel: 565280
Fax: 565989
E-mail: vsodir@africaonline.co.ke

Prof. Paschal B. Mihyo
Coordinator
African Technology Policy Studies Network
Liaison House, State House Avenue
PO Box 62084
Nairobi, Kenya
Tel: 713160
Fax: 711063
E-mail: pmihyo@idrc.ca

Ms Joy M. Mita
Administrative Secretary
African Technology Policy Studies
Liaison House, State House Avenue
PO Box 62084
Nairobi, Kenya
Tel: 713160
Fax: 711063
E-mail: jmita@idrc.or.ke

Dr William R. Mizray
Curator
National Herbarium of Tanzania
Tropical Pesticides Research Institute
PO Box 3024
Arusha, Tanzania
Tel: 057-8042
E-mail: tpri@yako.habari.co.tz


Mr Ali Mufuruki
Chair and Chief Executive Officer
Infotech Investment Group Ltd
PO Box 76686
Dar es Salaam, Tanzania
Tel: 051-117933-6
Fax: 051-118048
E-mail: infotech@raha.com


Ms Maria Mulei
Program Specialist
USAID Kenya
PO Box 30261
Nairobi, Kenya
Tel: 751613
Fax: 905094
E-mail: mmulei@usaid.gov


Mr Muriuki Mureithi
Director
Summit Strategies
PO Box 62454
Nairobi, Kenya
Tel: 788984
Fax: 226584
E-mail: summit@users.africaonline.co.ke


Mr Charles Musisi
Uganda Online – East Africa Help Desk
PO Box 12510
Kampala, Uganda
Tel: 041-233293
Fax: 041-233293
E-mail: cmusisi@uol.co.ug


Mr Douglas Mutembei
Communications Technician
Wilken AfSat (T) Ltd
PO Box 35192
Dar es Salaam, Tanzania
Tel: 051-865617
Fax: 051-865618
E-mail: douglas@wilken-dsm.com


Ms Edith K. Muthigani
Chief Science Secretary
National Council for Science and
    Technology
PO Box 30623
Nairobi, Kenya
Tel: 336173-76
Fax: 330947
E-mail: emuthigani@insightkenya.com


Ms Sheila Muthoni Mwai
Reinsurance Assistant
East Africa Reinsurance Co. Ltd
PO Box 34841
Nairobi, Kenya
E-mail: sheila.mwai@aig.com


Ms Virginia Ruguru Njoroge
Kenya Environmental Non Governmental
    Organisation
PO Box 45748
Nairobi, Kenya
Tel: 337826


Ms Edith Ofwona
Research Officer
International Development Research Centre
Liaison House, State House Avenue
PO Box 62084
Nairobi, Kenya
Tel: 713160
Fax: 711063
E-mail: eofwona@idrc.or.ke


Dr Osita Ogbu
Senior Program Specialist
International Development Research Centre
Liaison House, State House Avenue
PO Box 62084
Nairobi, Kenya
Tel: 713160
Fax: 711063
E-mail: oogbu@idrc.or.ke


Dr John Onunga
Chair
Information Technology Standards
    Association
PO Box 62994
Nairobi, Kenya
Tel: 228541
Fax: 219185
E-mail: isa@africaonline.co.ke

Dr H.M. Oranga
Biostatistician and Health Information
    System Specialist
African Medical Relief Foundation
Langata Road, Wilson Airport
PO Box 30125
Nairobi, Kenya
Tel: 501301
Fax: 506112
E-mail: amref.kco@amref.org

Mr Francis Odhiambo Ouma
Corporate Development
International Association of Students in
    Management and Economics – Kenya
c/o Dean of Students
University of Nairobi
PO Box 30197
Nairobi, Kenya
Tel: 245135
Fax: 211701
E-mail: aiesec_kenya@africaonline.co.ke

Mr Geoffrey Shimanyula
Product Manager
Africa Online (Kenya)
PO Box 52648
Nairobi, Kenya
Tel: 243775
Fax: 243762
E-mail: geoffrey@africaonline.co.ke

Mr Chris Wamalwa
Information and Media Relations Officer
NGO Council
PO Box 48278
Nairobi, Kenya
Tel: 574657
Fax: 574660
E-mail: ngocouncil@elci.sasa.unon.org

Mr Francis Mwaniki Weru
Assistant Chief Research Officer
Telkom Kenya Ltd
PO Box 48356
Nairobi, Kenya
Tel: 449374
Fax: 444482

## About the Institution

The International Development Research Centre (IDRC) is committed to building a sustainable and equitable world. IDRC funds developing-world researchers, thus enabling the people of the South to find their own solutions to their own problems. IDRC also maintains information networks and forges linkages that allow Canadians and their developing-world partners to benefit equally from a global sharing of knowledge. Through its actions, IDRC is helping others to help themselves.

## About the Publisher

IDRC Books publishes research results and scholarly studies on global and regional issues related to sustainable and equitable development. As a specialist in development literature, IDRC Books contributes to the body of knowledge on these issues to further the cause of global understanding and equity. IDRC publications are sold through its head office in Ottawa, Canada, as well as by IDRC's agents and distributors around the world. The full catalogue is available at http://www.idrc.ca/books/index.html.

## About the Authors

Osita Ogbu is Senior Program Specialist at the Nairobi office of Canada's International Development Research Centre.

Paschal Mihyo is a professor at the Institute of Social Studies in The Hague. He was formerly Coordinator of the African Technology Policy Studies Network, which is administered from the Nairobi office of Canada's International Development Research Centre.